WALKS FROM THE
WEST HIGHLAND RAILWAY

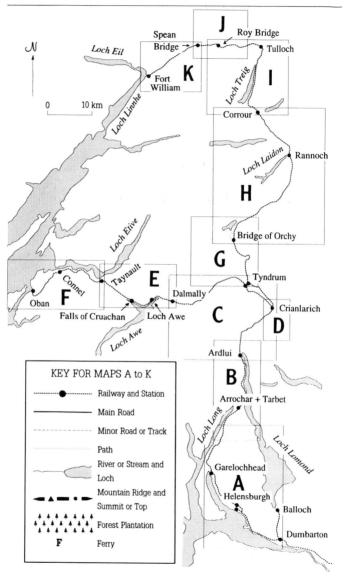

WALKS FROM THE
WEST HIGHLAND RAILWAY
including the ascent of 18 Munros

by

CHRIS AND JOHN HARVEY

CICERONE PRESS
MILNTHORPE, CUMBRIA

DEDICATION

*We should like to dedicate this book to all those native Scots
who have made us so welcome in their beautiful country*

ACKNOWLEDGEMENTS

We would like to thank Scotrail for supporting us in researching the walks
for this book. In particular we have appreciated the interest and
encouragement of Mr Bill Irwin, lately Promotions Manager, Scotrail. We
much appreciate the contributions made by Mike Harvey, not least the
painstaking production of graphics versions of the maps in the book. Many
individuals have given us helpful information about areas they know well
and we are especially grateful to Alec Cunnningham at Rannoch, Norman
Douglas and Bill Kinsey at Tarbet, Ian McVean at Dalmally, and Tom Rigg
at Corrour. In researching some of the walks we have enjoyed the company
of fellow members of the Glasgow Nordic Ski Club and of the Chamois
Mountaineering Club.

We are also pleased to be able to acknowledge assistance from many
landowners and estate managers, and from Dougal Roy, compiler of the
1993 edition of *Heading for the Scottish Hills.* We have gained much insight
from the Scottish Mountaineering Club publications and from the work of
such stalwarts as Tom Weir and Jimmie MacGregor. Inevitably there are
many others whose contributions have enriched this book but who are not
mentioned by name; to one and all our grateful thanks.

Chris & John Harvey
Tarbet House, Spring 1994

Front Cover: Loch Ossian looking north-east

CONTENTS

PART THREE: TYNDRUM to FORT WILLIAM

LIST OF MAPS

ADVICE TO READERS

Readers are advised that whilst every effort is taken by the authors to ensure the accuracy of this guidebook, changes can occur which may affect the contents. New fences and stiles appear, waymarking alters, there may be new buildings or eradication of old buildings. It is advisable to check locally on transport, accommodation, shops etc. but even rights of way can be altered, paths can be eradicated by landslip, forest clearances or change of ownership. The publisher would welcome notes of any such changes.

INTRODUCTION

The West Highland Railway, which opened in 1894, thus celebrating its Centenary in 1994 - the year of publication of this book, provides the walker with access to some of the finest mountains and scenery in Scotland. The original line ran from Craigendoran (on the Glasgow to Helensburgh line) to Fort William, a distance of 160km (100 miles); it was extended a further 60km (38 miles) to Mallaig in 1901. That section of the orignial Callander and Oban Railway from Crianlarich to Oban now serves as a branch line for the West Highland Line.

The Walks and a Little History

This book describes walks from stations on the lines from Helensburgh to Crianlarich (Part 1), from Crianlarich to Oban (Part 2) and from Tyndrum to Fort William (Part 3), hence they are (virtually) all possible to undertake with a day return ticket from Glasgow. One exception is perhaps the long walk from Bridge of Orchy to Rannoch via Kingshouse where the walker can get overnight accommodation in the hotel.

Ranging from ascents of Munros (mountains over 3000ft ie. 914m - there are 277 of them in Scotland), to long routes using remote valleys and mountain passes, and shorter, mostly level, walks there is invariably something to attract the reader to sample the splendid lochs and glens and awe-inspiring peaks and moors of the West Highlands at first hand.

It is difficult for us to pick out a favourite among the walks - it is usually the one we have just done - but the high point of the line is certainly Corrour Station, at 400m (1340ft) above sea level the highest station not only on the West Highland Line but also in the whole of the rail network in the British Isles. Corrour is accessible only by rail or on foot, the nearest roads being some 12km away. It is a magical place...but many other delights also await the West Highland Rail traveller who enjoys walking. He or she will be following a long tradition; in the days before widespread car ownership the early mountaineering pioneers made great use of the railway to reach these mountains.

The Scottish Mountaineering Club (SMC) was established in 1889 and some of its first Meets were held in the vicinity of Tyndrum, it being already served by a railway. Thus many climbs on Ben Lui were pioneered between 1891 and 1896. SMC members were planning to explore major routes on Ben Nevis after the railway reached Fort William in 1894, but in the meantime a party led by J.Norman Collie made the first complete ascent of the Tower Ridge in March 1894. The SMC held Easter meets at Fort William in 1895 and in 1896 when a special saloon carriage took members there from Glasgow; the climbers' guide to Ben Nevis records a number of first ascents including Castle Ridge during these two Meets.

Between the two World Wars a new breed of climber was active in the Arrochar Alps, particularly on The Cobbler, readily accessible from Arrochar & Tarbet Station, and the first meet of the Junior Mountaineering Club of Scotland was held in the 1920s at the Narnain Boulders (see Walk 6).

It was 1891 when Sir Hugh Munro first published a Table of Munros, and 1901 when the first Munroist, the Reverend A.E.Robertson, relying on trains and steamers for access to the mountains, completed the ascent of all those summits over 3000ft. Since then "Munro-bagging" has become a very popular preoccupation with hillwalkers. 52 Munro summits lie within 10km of stations on the West Highland Line, and the walks described in this book include the ascent of 18 of these; the aspiring Munroist will no doubt be able to find routes up most of the others from the nearest station.

Be Prepared

To enable assessment of the demands of a particular walk we have graded each one and before the description of each walk there is a **Route Review** summary of distance, ascent, terrain etc. Grades (see below) are, however, subjective and can only be relative; what may be easy to the walker who is experienced on the Scottish hills may be a major expedition for someone who has only previously walked in lowland Britain, and a walk which we have graded moderate may become an epic struggle even for an experienced walker in severe weather conditions - it is recorded that in December 1973 it took a climber 22 hours to reach the Charles Inglis Clark Hut from the Ben Nevis Distillery (Walk 40.) On a first visit to this part of Scotland it would be wise to start with a walk of a lower grade than you might tackle elsewhere until experience is gained.

Equipment and Maps

Hence it is most important that walkers are equipped for all the vagaries of the Scottish weather - particularly in remoter areas or where a station may have no waiting room, and that those undertaking moderate and difficult walks as well as serious mountain expeditions are properly equipped with mountain gear - boots, waterproof outer clothing, compass, map (1:50,000 Ordnance Survey Landranger) and rucksack with spare clothing and survival bag, first aid kit and food. Winter in Scotland needs to be taken seriously; arctic conditions often prevail and what may be an easy grassy slope in summer can transform into a lethal ice slide in winter, so ice axes and crampons are needed for going onto the hills and mountains in winter. Avalanches can and do occur in Scotland and they lead to fatalities in most winters; beware of snow-covered slopes of 25 to 45 degrees particularly after a rapid build-up of snow or a sudden temperature rise, or if they have a convex profile, and obtain avalanche reports (issued for the Lochaber area around Fort William from December to April).

We have included 11 maps in this guide to show the routes which we describe, but these should be considered only as sketch maps. In the descriptions we assume that the walker will be using maps of a scale 1:50,000 (Ordnance Survey Landranger) or greater, as listed in the Route Reviews; in general names of places and rivers are shown on these maps. Occasionally we give six-figure grid references to assist in the identification of a point on the map; those not familiar with such references will find an explanation and example in the key to any Landranger map.

Skills

It is not sufficient to have adequate equipment if you do not know how to use it! This applies to ice axe and crampons in winter, but especially to map and compass at all times. It cannot be stressed too much that those venturing into the Scottish mountain areas should know how to use their map and compass. In general compass directions given in the descriptions of walks are cardinal and compass points only (N, S, E, W, NE, SSW, etc.) rather than bearings and are intended only to assist you in identifying the route on the map. They are not a substitute for you taking your own bearings with map and compass when visibility is restricted and the route ahead is not clear. Begin to use your compass when you still know where you are - if you wait until you are already lost or in cloud you have made navigation infinitely more difficult.

Remember the mist can come down at any time, it can snow even in summer and, what may be a pleasant day as you set off in calm weather near sea level, can turn into a howling gale on a 1000m summit at any time of year. Needless to say in researching the walks we also experienced less than optimum weather at times so not every walk has detailed descriptions of views to delight the eye - but you may sometimes be more fortunate than we were!

Some Technical Details

i) Grading of Walks

a) Easy: a relatively straightforward walk on a well-surfaced track or path with few route-finding problems

b) Moderate: usually some uphill climb and paths may be rough or muddy in places

c) Difficult: a challenging, long and often strenuous walk in remote country; may involve navigation skills as there are not always paths to follow. For experienced and well-equipped hill walkers

d) Serious: a serious mountain expedition involving the ascent of one or more mountains and traversing terrain without paths, with all that entails for navigation skills and equipment

In the following walk descriptions "tracks" are generally of firm construction and wide (enough to take a vehicle) though usually unsurfaced. "Paths" or "footpaths" are narrow and may be stony or muddy, being routes usually made by walkers themselves and they may be indistinct in places (eg. where walkers have spread out laterally).

ii) Lengths and Distances

These are given in metric units - kilometres (km), with a conversion to miles for total length in the Route Review, and metres. Heights are also given in metres. Note that in the text **the abbreviation m** refers to a vertical height whereas **metres** refers to a horizontal distance. Such metric measurements are consistent with using the Ordnance Survey Landranger and Pathfinder Maps. Distance information given within the walk description (or measured on the map) can be estimated by the walker over the ground by counting paces; whilst the conversion of paces to distance varies from one person to another and with the nature of the terrain, on level ground a typical conversion would be: 130 paces (or 65 double paces) = approximately 100 metres.

iii) Times

The time taken to complete a walk will vary very much from one party to another, so we have left it for you to estimate these for yourself from the distance, ascent and terrain given in the Route Review. Naismith's rule is widely used which allows one hour for every 3 miles (5km) plus 1/2 hour for every 1000 ft (300m), but this was formulated for "men in fair condition for easy expeditions" and allowed no time for any stops. You will almost certainly want to add to this time for lunch stops and rests and to allow more time for rough terrain and for any members of your party who are not what a fit mountaineer would describe as being in "fair condition".

Climate and Weather

There is considerable regional variation in the climate within Scotland. The figures quoted here are averages for measurements taken at Onich, at sea level and a short distance from Fort William, and come from *The Climate of Scotland - some facts and figures*, HMSO.

i) **Rainfall:** driest months: April (111mm) May (103mm) June (124mm);

wettest months: October - January (over 200mm) (1 inch = 25.4mm)

ii) **Temperature** (degrees Celsius): the warmest month, July, has average monthly maximum and minimum temperatures of

23°C and 4°C, whilst the corresponding values for the coldest month, January, are 11°C and - 6°C

iii) **Daily sunshine** hours range from December 0.6 to May 5.3

Note: short winter days are offset by long summer days with sunrise around 04.30 and sunset around 22.30 on 21st June

You should note that the area of the walks is subject to very local weather conditions and to rapid weather changes brought about by fronts and depressions coming in from the Atlantc. There is usually a marked change in weather conditions with height: wind speed increases, often being particularly strong on exposed ridges and cols where it is funnelled through them, precipitation increases, cloud is encountered and temperature decreases. Evaporation, promoted by wind, leads to "wind chill", but in addition to this temperature may well decrease at a rate of as much as 1°C for every 100m of ascent. Exposure to wind chill, particularly in wet conditions, can lead to hypothermia, and the mountain walker should be able to recognise the early symptoms and know the appropriate action and treatment for this.

The mountains can also make accurate detailed forecasting very difficult, however -

LOCAL WEATHER FORECASTS FOR THE AREA
MAY BE OBTAINED FROM
WEATHERCALL ON   0891 500 421
(After April 16 1995 area code changes to 01891)

Geology and Landscape

Within the area served by the West Highland Railway are some of the most spectacular mountains of Scotland including Ben Nevis, the highest mountain in Britain. The region is, however, deeply dissected, and it is the mixture of mountains and lochs, both freshwater and fiord-like sea lochs, which gives this area north of the Highland Boundary Fault its special characteristics.

The geological structure dates back to the Caledonian Mountain building period some 400 to 500 million years ago. During this episode the sedimentary rocks were deformed and folded, and sandstones, shales and gritstone were metamorphosed by heat and pressure to form quartzites, slates and schists. Meanwhile molten rock formed at the base of the mountain chain; part of this cooled within the Earth's crust to form great masses of granite whilst part was extruded at the surface in lava flows. Some of the granite intrusions are tough and resistant to erosion such as those comprising Ben Cruachan, whilst others are weak such as that beneath Rannoch Moor. Ben Nevis reveals the remnants of volcanoes which are thought to have sunk into inner granite whilst the lava was still liquid when the roof of a subterranean cauldron collapsed, thus protecting the lava from erosion. The original Caledonian Mountains were gradually planed down and, about 60 million years ago (in Tertiary times), following further uplift, it is thought that most of Scotland sloped down to the east with rivers draining in this direction.

Most of the landscape we see today, however, is the result of erosion by ice and glaciers during the last million years. There were a series of glacial and inter-glacial periods during this time, but evidence shows that ice and glaciers were widespread in the Western Highlands as recently as 10,000 years ago during the so-called Loch Lomond Re-advance. The main site of ice accumulation in the glacial periods was in the vicinity of Rannoch Moor; from there it escaped through the surrounding mountains as glaciers, carving troughs as much as 600m deep, radiated outwards from the centre of ice accumulation, breaching the pre-existing drainage system and creating a new pattern. Much evidence is to be seen of this glacial erosion: steep-sided or U-shaped valleys, thus truncating the previous ridges, and often containing deep rock basins now filled by lochs; corries predominantly facing north-east in which ice accumulated and which now often contain lochans. Also evident are features of deposition by glaciers: moraines and drumlins such as those near Tyndrum, and erratics such as those strewn across Rannoch Moor; other features are associated with the meltwaters which emanated from them: meltwater channels and terraces, shorelines of ice-dammed lakes as in Glen Roy, ridges of sand and gravel (eskers), and depressions (kettles), as seen between Fersit and Tulloch.

Access

Much has been said and written about the often vexed question of access to the countryside and particularly to the mountain areas of Scotland.

Rights of way are of much less significance in Scotland than in England and Wales as they are not shown on Ordnance Survey maps and there is no requirement for local authorities to list or map them. Hence there is much dispute in deciding which routes have right of way status.

Scottish Natural Heritage published a consultation paper on access entitled *Enjoying the Outdoors* in December 1992 with a view to developing policies for open air recreation. Meanwhile bodies such as the Ramblers Association and the Mountaineering Council of Scotland emphasise the freedom to roam over Scottish hills which has evolved through custom and tradition, and seek to have this right to roam in open country formally recognised. The Scottish Landowners' Federation in their review of access (1990) resist the use of legislation to resolve issues of access, but support all measures aimed at achieving "responsible access to the countryside" through goodwill and balanced compromise.

The mountain environment is fragile: trampling can damage sensitive vegetation, some species of wildlife can be at risk from disturbance, and footpath erosion is a major problem in some areas. We must seek to ensure that our natural heritage is not impaired for the future. In addition it must be appreciated that the countryside is in demand not only for recreation but also constitutes the working environment in the Highlands. Therefore walkers should be sensitive and reponsive to activities taking place.

The Mountaineering Council of Scotland, together with the Scottish Landowners' Federation, acknowledge that a basic freedom of access to the hills carries a responsibility to try to avoid disrupting and disturbing wildlife, field sports such as stalking (the stalking season runs from mid August to the third week in October when the stags are culled, whilst the culling of hinds may continue until February) and farming activities such as lambing in April and May. They have jointly published a handbook entitled *Heading for the Scottish Hills* which contains information about estate ownership with names and telephone numbers for making contact at critical times of year to find out what activities are occurring. We commend this handbook; much of the information on estates in our Route

Reviews and Appendix comes from it. Therefore walkers should take heed of requests to avoid certain areas in the stalking season (not least for their own safety!). Sheep and lambs should be given a wide berth and dogs be left at home during the lambing season and kept under control at other times unless prohibited.

A further safety matter should be emphasised. While trespass is not, in general, a criminal offence there are certain situations where it is prohibited under specific legislation. One such case relates to railway lines. Not only is it trespassing to walk along the railway, it is also foolhardy in the extreme; every year people are killed on railway lines and that includes the West Highland Line which carries significantly more traffic than in the scheduled timetable. Fatalities to walkers have occurred when trains approaching from behind are not heard, perhaps during strong winds. You have been warned!

The Country Code

Enjoy the countryside and respect its life and work
Guard against all risk of fire
Take your litter home
Fasten all gates
Help to keep all water clean
Keep your dogs under close control
Protect wildlife, plants and trees
Keep to public paths across farmland
Take special care on country roads
Leave livestock, crops and machinery alone
Make no unnecessary noise
Use gates and stiles to cross fences, hedges and walls

Wee Beasties and other hindrances

From the end of May until September this area of Scotland is prey to the midge and so too will the walker be prey unless avoiding action is taken.

If they are troublesome, typically in damp weather and poor lighting conditions, then full arm and leg cover will reduce the areas available for attack and repellant creams and sprays are advisable. The best prevention, however is to keep moving as midges do not seem to summon up the energy to keep up with you and bite.

It is as well to be aware also that ticks from sheep and deer are present in this area and can attach themselves to the unwary walker if in need of a feed. If, on inspection, you find one has attached itself to you, one method of removal is by applying a hot (extinguished) match to it and pulling it out in its entirety with tweezers. Ticks can transmit Lyme disease to humans which can be serious but is readily treatable so if, after removal of a tick, reddening persists, a rash appears or you develop 'flu-like symptoms you should see your doctor.

From about May to September bracken becomes widespread on some of the hillsides in the southern part of our area and, unless you can find a path made by other walkers or perhaps by sheep, progress can be very slow.

Accommodation, Refreshments and Travel

Hotel, guest house and bed & breakfast accommodation is very plentiful in the area but in the summer months it is also very popular; during this period, and in remote areas, it is wise to book ahead. Tourist information centres (see Appendix B) can assist with advice and bookings.

Simple accommodation can be obtained in Scottish youth hostels and bunkhouses and primitive shelter is available to the self-sufficient backpacker in mountain bothies in remote areas (eg. over the Lairig Leacach).

The refreshment information given in the Route Reviews relates to what may be available at the end of a walk, or sometimes on route; we do not mention provision at the start except for Walk 32 where there are only refreshments at Rannoch and nothing at Corrour.

Rail travel has many advantages: it enables linear walks, starting and finishing at different stations, and it is distinctly more environmentally friendly than travel by car. Trains run regularly from Glasgow Queen Street station, more frequently during the summer than in winter. It may be however that the walker in the Western Highlands would be better based within reach of Arrochar & Tarbet or Crianlarich Stations so as to take advantage of a period "runabout" ticket. At the time of writing the Sunday service was fairly minimal but perhaps pressure from walkers will bring about recognition by Scotrail of the level of demand for more Sunday trains. Times and other details are not given here as they are subject to change from year to year so you should consult your local station, travel agent or, at the time of writing: Scotrail, Caledonian Chambers, 87 Union Street, Glasgow, G1 3TA

The West Highland Line passes through the most spectacular scenery guaranteed to tempt you to set foot. Enjoy!

INTRODUCTION

The West Highland Railway leaves the Glasgow to Helensburgh line at Craigendoran which is located almost exactly at the position where the Highland Boundary Fault, separating the Highlands from the Central Valley of Scotland, reaches the Firth of Clyde. In this first part of the book we cover walks from stations between Helensburgh and Crianlarich, where the West Highland Line once crossed the Caledonian Line which ran from Callandar to Oban.

Our first walk takes us across the Highland Boundary Fault to Balloch at the southern end of Loch Lomond, but then we move northwards via Garelochhead into the Luss Hills and on to the Arrochar Alps, reached from Arrochar & Tarbet. The railway now follows a delightful route along the west side of Loch Lomond and we have walks from Ardlui, one involving a ferry, through Glen Falloch and on to the Munros to the east of this Glen.

1. HELENSBURGH to DUMBARTON via BALLOCH

SEE MAP A p22

ROUTE REVIEW

Stations:	Helensburgh Upper, Dumbarton Central
Distance:	i) Helensburgh to Balloch: 12km (7½ miles); 220m ascent
	ii) Balloch to Dumbarton: 10km (6 miles); no ascent
Grade:	i) Moderate (but route finding is not easy)
	ii) Easy
Maps:	OS Landrangers 56 & 63; OS Pathfinder (1:25,000) NS 28/38
Terrain:	i) follows paths (often wet) and crosses open moor;
	ii) follows the well-surfaced Leven Towpath and is suitable for bikes
Estates:	Luss; Bannachra Muir
Refreshments:	Balloch and Dumbarton - plenty of choice

NB. Either part i) or part ii) can be walked separately using Balloch Station on the suburban network

i) HELENSBURGH to BALLOCH

Helensburgh, dubbed the "Brighton of Glasgow" at the turn of the century, was a fashionable town founded on the Clyde estuary in 1777 by Sir James Colquhoun in honour of his wife, Helen. Its many elegant houses were occupied by merchants and the town is still popular with commuters to Glasgow. The Upper Station lies on the West Highland Railway and is the starting point for a varied route over the moors to Balloch and then alongside the River Leven to Dumbarton. There is an Upland Way planned between Helensburgh and Balloch which should produce a waymarked route; meanwhile the route finding required for the walk described here may be assisted with use of the OS Pathfinder (1:25,000) NS 28/38 map.

* * *

From Helensburgh Upper Station turn right down Sinclair Street (B832) which leads into Helensburgh affording a good view across the Clyde, and then second left into East Abercrombie Street. After some 600 metres this tree-lined road crosses the railway line and 150 metres after the railway bridge Golfhill Drive forks right; turn right along it and past a couple of side roads until you reach some council housing and, on the right, a cul-de-sac called Fisher Place. On the left, opposite Fisher Place, there is a green track between the houses and a wooden fence and wall. Follow this track, the route of the old Luss road, up and over the golf course and into a wood to reach a gate (GR 314836). Go through the gate and turn right alongside the fence. Here the route becomes tussocky and can be wet. Pass beneath a pylon line and continue in the same general direction (E) following an old wall with a fence alongside. You will find that in places the foundations of the wall provide the driest route.

At the corner of a new plantation on the right, with Bannachra (birch) Woods to the left, cross into the plantation - there is a Fire Danger (Tilhill) sign - and follow along the left edge to cross a burn before reaching a new forest road. Continue right along this road (which has come up from the B832) with a burn on your right,

MAP A

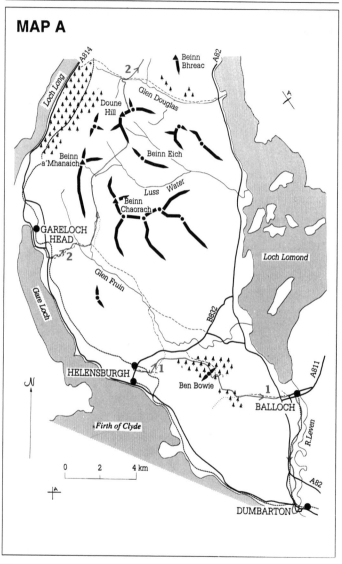

through new plantation, mainly spruce but intermixed with larch and pine, heading ESE uphill to the shoulder of Ben Bowie.

Splendid views open up across Loch Lomond and its islands with the pronounced feature of Conic Hill on the opposite shore of the Loch signalling the line of the Highland Boundary Fault which threads its way across the islands, and the separation of the Highlands from the Central Valley of Scotland. By way of confirmation that the Highlands are at hand, the massive bulk of Ben Lomond, Scotland's most southerly Munro, (Scottish mountain over 3000 feet), presides majestically over the Loch.

After a little over 1km the forest road divides; take the right-hand fork which continues to ascend and follows round the hillside before crossing a major burn. At another fork again keep right and then swing right to keep Gouk Hill (275m spot height on OS map 56) on your left. The forest road begins to descend a scarp slope, on the line of the Highland Boundary Fault, affording brief views across the Firth of Clyde. Where the road comes to an end head steeply downhill and towards the right (SE) to reach a fence corner. Cross over and head ESE over tussocky heather moor crossed by sheep tracks, keeping a fence and plantation on your right.

Some 1¹/4km further on cross a ruined wall and then a double fence enabling you to continue in the same direction for a further 250 metres to reach Stoneymollan Muir, a delightful green track offering firm going underfoot. This leads downhill with views over Balloch, your immediate destination, and Jamestown. After Upper Stoneymollan on the left the road becomes metalled and descends a wooded glen to cross the A82 by a footbridge. Continue on down the lane past Drumkinnon Farm to the old road. Turn right here and then left at the garage in 200 metres to follow the main road to Balloch Tourist Information Centre, housed in the old station buildings, across the road from the new station.

ii) BALLOCH to DUMBARTON

The small town of Balloch marks the gateway to Loch Lomond and straddles the River Leven which drains from the loch and reaches the River Clyde via a meandering route of some 12¹/2km (8 miles) at Dumbarton, a mere 8km as the seagull flies. Balloch Station is not on the West Highland Railway line but forms a terminus on the Glasgow suburban network. Trains on both this suburban network

River Leven at Dumbarton

and the West Highland Line stop at Dumbarton Central.

*   *   *

From Balloch Tourist Information Centre make your way to the riverside, on the N side of Balloch Bridge (built in 1842), and join the towpath which follows the western bank of the River Leven on its course downstream to Dumbarton. Pass beneath the two road bridges carrying the traffic through Balloch above the many moored boats in the Leven, often a subject for visiting artists. You will shortly reach the Leven Barrage, built in 1971 to control the water level in Loch Lomond in connection with its use as a reservoir for the Central Valley of Scotland.

The towpath, which up to 100 years ago was used by horses towing scows (flat-bottomed boats) up the river to Loch Lomond, is now a well-surfaced cycle track and walkway. One of the adjacent buildings on your right houses the Loch Lomond Rowing Club. With the demise of much of the traditional industries such as bleaching, dyeing and textile printing in the Vale of Leven new industrial estates have grown up causing less environmental pressure on the river area and a consequent increase in wildlife. If you are very fortunate you may see otters or mink but you will almost certainly see water birds and anglers each perhaps hoping for trout or salmon.

Once underneath an old railway bridge, now pedestrianised,

you reach more open green land interspersed with industrial works and units. Beyond Jamestown, home to Bartons Distillery, there is a bend in the river at Alexandria with picnic tables. Continue on and under Bonhill Bridge (1837), which was a toll bridge until 1895, into a more urban area with views of hills to the right above the houses. Beyond the Vale of Leven Academy, and after passing under Dillichip Bridge (1875), the river meanders around a loop for about 1km but there is a short cut taking you more directly on through Renton. There is a further loop and short cut beyond Renton and this stretch marks the tidal limits of the River Leven, just upstream of Ballantine's Distillery. As the river winds around the Ballantines bend the tall trees on the east bank contrast with the open meadow and reeds on the west side.

Continue along the towpath, crossing two rustic bridges built in 1982 by a Youth Opportunities Programme team and pass under the dual carriageway (A82). Fork left (signed as a right of way) across a cattle grid (or through an adjacent gate) on a well-constructed track raised above the reed bed. Continue on to rejoin the ever-widening river, popular here with fishermen often thigh-deep in the water, towards Dumbarton with the Rock, some 80m of basalt known as the "Gibraltar of the Clyde", and Castle coming into view amongst the buildings. Pass under the railway bridge and new road bridge, continuing on alongside the moored boats to old Dumbarton bridge. Take the track up to it and turn left across the bridge.

Dumbarton Central Station is ahead and to your left, and can be reached by crossing the dual carriageway and then turning right. The station overlooks Dumbarton Common (originally "Broadmeadow") which used to flood regularly at high tide but the building of an embankment to contain the River Leven has enabled reclamation of the land.

2. GARELOCHHEAD to ARROCHAR & TARBET
over DOUNE HILL (734m)

SEE MAPS A p22 & B p27

ROUTE REVIEW

Stations: Garelochhead, Arrochar & Tarbet
Distance: 24km (15 miles); 1290m ascent

Grade:	Difficult/Serious
Map:	OS Landranger 56
Terrain:	some roads and tracks but mostly rugged moor and steep grass, wet in places without paths
Estate:	Luss
Refreshments:	Tarbet - The Black Sheep Restaurant

The route from Garelochhead to Arrochar & Tarbet through and over the Luss Hills passes through a remote and largely trackless area where you are unlikely to meet another soul once you've left Glen Fruin. **Although we have graded this walk as Difficult/ Serious it should certainly be regarded as a Serious Hill Walk.** The attraction is solitude and splendid views but the expedition requires self-sufficiency and sound navigation skills. The northern part of the walk is over Ant-Sreang, a pass between Glen Douglas and Arrochar, reputedly used by the MacFarlane Clan to reach their church in Luss - a safer passage than along the forested Loch Lomondside.

The southern area has had a chequered history: Glen Fruin, known as "glen of sorrows", was the scene of repeated feuds between Clan Colquhoun and Clan McGregor, of which more later. The Glen once supported a large crofting community and as this became unviable the inhabitants turned to smuggling and illicit whisky distilling. Depopulation ensued when the excisemen caught up with the activity! Today the main activity in the area is that carried out by the Ministry of Defence (MOD). Nowadays however the Luss Hills' sheep far outnumber their human inhabitants; indeed the area is somewhat notorious for its role in changing Scottish history. 1749 saw the introduction here of black-faced sheep and anticipation of lucrative rewards from sheep farming led to the landowners' Highland Clearances with evictions and large scale emigration during the following century. The sheep also consolidated vegetation change as their grazing prevented regeneration of the trees already felled by man.

Garelochhead Station sits above the town which marks the head of Gare Loch, ("the short loch" from the Gaelic - *gerr*), a northern finger of the Clyde estuary. The loch, deemed to be free of localised magnetic influence, was used for testing ships' compasses.

* * *

MAP B

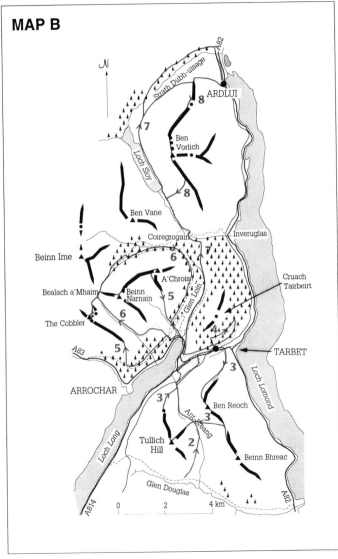

Strath Dubh-uisage

A82

ARDLUI 8

7

Loch Sloy

Ben Vorlich

8

Ben Vane

Coiregrogain

Inveruglas

Beinn Ime

7

6

A'Chrois

Cruach Tairbeirt

Bealach a'Mhaim

Beinn Narnain

5

Glen Loin

The Cobbler

6

5

4

TARBET

A83

5

Loch Lomond

ARROCHAR

3

Loch Long

3

Ben Reoch

An t-Sreang

3

Tullich Hill

2

Beinn Bhreac

A814

Glen Douglas

0   2   4 km

A82

Turn left out of the station and follow the road round a sharp right-hand bend. Just before the road swings left again, turn left down some steps along a footpath, which is a right of way, to join a minor road which services some houses and thence to the road alongside the loch, emerging near to the pier. *The predecessor to this pier was the scene of a battle in 1853 when the local laird, James Colquhoun, disapproving of Sunday sailings, attempted to prevent a pleasure steamer from berthing only to be met by fierce retaliation from the crew in the form of vegetable missiles and flying crockery.*

Follow the A814 S along the lochside using the pavement on the right-hand side. Passing the MOD fencing - the MOD is a major employer here - you will reach a roundabout shortly after passing a sign to a cemetery on the left. Turn right at the roundabout and after 100 metres take the left turn up Glen Fruin Road. Follow this as it snakes uphill for about 2km. You will pass Strone House. *This was the site of a cattle raid on the Colquhouns by the McGregors in 1527 so fierce that Mary Queen of Scots issued "Letters of Fire and Sword" against Clan McGregor in 1563. Nevertheless the Clan battles continued to rage, a group of divinity student onlookers being slaughtered in one fray.*

After crossing a cattle grid and a bridge (over Fruin Water) you reach a private road going off to the left (GR 274900). Turn left along this road, owned by Strathclyde Water Authority and leading up to a dam. After some 200 metres the road crosses what, at the time of writing, is a private MOD road. Continue on, heading N, until the road ends at the dam where your route goes through the trees on the E side of the reservoir. There is a faint path to follow (about 100 metres E of the burn) which leads onwards through the ruins of some shielings - relics of earlier grazing practices when cattle were taken to higher pastures for summer grazing - to a col or "bealach" at about 350m. Cross this watershed to the N side of the burn flowing down the other side and head downhill, bearing left (NE) to cross the upper reaches of Luss Water at GR 287947.

Your main steep climb towards Doune Hill lies ahead to gain the ridge between Beinn Eich and Beinn Lochain, but this can be eased by zigzagging and using the terraces and watercourses which slope mainly from left to right and can be seen as kinks in the contours on the 1:25,000 OS map. *Perhaps these features were left by melting ice at the close of the glacial period some 10,000 years ago since they seem unrelated to present drainage patterns.* As the gradient eases continue on to the crest of the ridge at, or slightly left of, the col at GR 295954 and turn left (NNW), following the ridge for about 1km to a small pile of stones on the grassy summit of Beinn Lochan.

A faint path leads ahead, down and swinging right, past a tiny lochan and then up, NE to a trig point which marks the summit of Doune Hill (hill of the black water). (If there are strong winds from the west, shelter can be found at the foot of a little crag about 100 metres ESE of the summit.) The descent from here is over steepish broken ground to a lochan at a bealach; in poor visibility you should use a compass course to take you ENE.

From the lochan ascend the slope ahead to a summit at 700m where there is a small cairn. Descent from here requires care: head NNW downhill for just less than 1km and then swing round to the right. The ground is steep with cliffs and a deep cleft. Pass below this and continue to descend diagonally right to pass just above the SE corner of a major fence around MOD property and continue down between the fence and a burn. To reach the road it is necessary to cross Douglas Water; a bridge at GR 295991 can be reached by following the MOD fence around to the left.

Turn right along the road for about 100 metres and then, after crossing a burn, head left up the slope towards a gate at a fence junction. Beyond the gate continue round the hill, ascending gradually; at first there is a drainage ditch to follow. A massive boulder is passed on the right, and the ground is boggy in parts, but continue round the hill still gaining height to reach a gate in a fence some 200 metres W of the burn which flows down to Invergroin. Still traversing round the hillside, aim towards the summit of Ben Reoch ahead to converge with the burn where there are a few trees growing, just above a set of meanders, in order to keep on drier ground. Now follow the burn to the summit of Ant-Sreang, most easily with the water on your left, as it tumbles down over the rocks.

As you reach the summit a dramatic view opens out ahead: the craggy outline of The Cobbler with Beinn Narnain on its right, peaks which are attained in Walk 5. The watershed is somewhat boggy, despite the many drainage ditches hereabouts, but as you proceed down towards Arrochar the angle steepens and the ground is better drained; the best ground is found along the right side of the burn.

Soon A'Chrois comes into view, connected to Beinn Narnain by the fine ridge above Creag Tharsuinn (Walk 5) and then Ben Vorlich (Walk 8) to its right and the hamlet of Succoth at the head of Loch Long.

On reaching trees and seeing Arrochar below and the disused torpedo testing station on the other side of Loch Long, leave the burn and head away to the right. There is an underpass beneath the railway at GR 298035 which gives access to a route down through Tighness woods to Arrochar church, where you turn right up Church Road to reach the A83; however the more direct route to Arrochar & Tarbet Station continues round the hillside and above the railway for about ³/₄km to a sheepfold where there is a bridge over the railway. From this bridge a track leads down to the main (A83) road, and turning right here it is only another ¹/₂km or so to the station.

3. BEN REOCH (661m), BEINN BHREAC (681m) and TULLICH HILL (632m) from ARROCHAR & TARBET

SEE MAP B p27

ROUTE REVIEW

Station:	Arrochar & Tarbet
Distance:	15km (9¹/₂ miles); 1030m ascent
Grade:	Difficult/Serious
Maps:	OS Landranger 56; OS Pathfinder (1:25,000) NN 20/30
Terrain:	steep and generally grassy hills without footpaths
Estate:	Luss
Refreshments:	Tarbet - The Black Sheep Restaurant

NB. There are two opportunities to shorten the walk described here:
a) Beinn Bhreac can be omitted, reducing the distance by 2¹/₂km and the ascent by 160m
b) Tullich Hill can be omitted, returning directly to the station from Ant-Sreang by the route of Walk 2; this reduces the distance by a little over 2km and the ascent by 270m

These are grand hills which give a feeling of wildness and offer excellent views of the surrounding mountains and of the lochs below. There is a marked absence of footpaths, so navigation is important, particularly in poor weather; it should be regarded as a **serious hill walk** even though the summits are all below 700m. This is all a sheep farming area and dogs should not be taken; particular care should be taken not to disturb the livestock, particularly during the lambing season (April and May).

*　*　*

From Arrochar & Tarbet Station take the minor road to the left to join the A83 outside the old Tarbet church (now the Black Sheep restaurant). *Behind here are reputedly some Viking graves dating back to the thirteenth century when King Haco's Norsemen lost their lives in plundering raids as they dragged their boats across from Loch Long to Loch Lomond. Also buried here in an annex are believed to be labourers who expired during the building of the West Highland Railway in the 1890s.*

Proceed down the A83 for about 250 metres to a gate on the S side of the road, through which there is a way onto the hill between a burn on the right and a wall on the left. This burn is followed for more than 1km to its source. Where the slope steepens, bracken will be encountered in summer; it is best avoided by a detour to the left, rejoining the burn at a distinct bend where the upward direction becomes SW. *Ben Lomond dominates the view to the left, and behind is a good view of the hamlet of Tarbet by the side of Loch Lomond. The Cobbler comes into view on the right with other adjacent Arrochar Alps.*

When the source of the burn is reached, continue in the same general direction, climbing steadily below the steep slope on the left. Head gradually to the left (S), and after about $^3/_4$km you will reach an old wall, at first overgrown and hardly discernible, but becoming very much more apparent where it crosses a small col. This wall leads almost to the summit of Ben Reoch - the cairn is just above and to the right of the wall's highest point - which provides excellent views all around and particularly of the further hills included in this walk.

From the summit descend towards the SE, passing a small marshy lochan. On the descent to the bealach between Ben Reoch and Beinn Bhreach there are two hillocks which can best be traversed round on their W sides. There are good views now across Glen Douglas of Doune Hill (Walk 2) and of some of the other Luss Hills.

From the bealach at about 525m, which is wet and peaty, the ridge leading S and then SSE is followed for about 1¹/₄km to the trig point on the summit of Beinn Bhreac (the speckled mountain). From here the many islands in the southern part of Loch Lomond are very well seen.

Return now to the bealach, looking towards Ben Reoch with Ben Vorlich (Walk 8) beyond on its right and The Cobbler (Walk 5) to its left. As the bealach is reached head left, just N of W, descending gradually as the steep slope is traversed and crossing a series of burns flowing towards Glen Douglas.

The goal is now the summit of Ant-Sreang, a pass between Arrochar and Glen Douglas (see Walk 2), and some 150m below the bealach, but the straight line to it passes through two crags, so you need to decide to go either above or below them.

From Ant-Sreang a steep grassy ridge with a line of cliffs on its left side will be seen leading SW; this provides a good route to the summit plateau of Tullich Hill, but its crest is not easily reached as the end of it is steep and rocky. However, an easier way up will be found about 100 metres round to the left. The summit of Tullich Hill, marked by a cairn, is on the far (SW) side of this plateau area, and again provides good views all round but now including that down Loch Long towards the Firth of Clyde.

The descent from the summit is to the north, initially down a steep slope, but then across a series of flat and wet stretches through which drainage ditches have been dug, to reach the trig point (447m) 1¹/₂km from Tullich Hill's cairn. From here one looks down onto Arrochar and Succoth at the head of Loch Long with distant views across Cruach Tairbeirt to the peaks between Glen Falloch and Balquidder.

To descend from here head NE to reach the southern end of the trees in the valley below; again the descent is steep, and though the slope is mainly grassy there are some small crags which are not easily seen from above. On reaching the trees the burn should be crossed without difficulty - below here it flows down a small gorge and the crossing is less easy. From here there are two alternative ways back to the station, described at the end of Walk 2: **either** use the underpass beneath the railway at GR 298035 and descend to Arrochar church through Tighness woods, turning right up Church

The Cobbler from above Arrochar (5, 6, 7)
Falls of Falloch (9)

Ben More and Cruach Ardrain (12) from Strath Fillan (13)
Approaching Ben Lui (15) from Cononish (14)

Road to reach the A83, or traverse round the hill above the railway to a sheepfold at GR 305039 and cross the railway by the bridge here.

4. CRUACH TAIRBEIRT FOREST WALK from ARROCHAR & TARBET

SEE MAP B p27

ROUTE REVIEW

Station:	Arrochar & Tarbet
Distance:	4km (2½ miles); 130m ascent
Grade:	Easy
Map:	OS Landranger 56
Terrain:	well-constructed footpath, but with some steep sections
Estate:	Argyll Forest Park - please do not use mountain bikes on this track
Refreshments:	Tarbet - The Black Sheep Restaurant

NB. This walk can be extended by following the footpath to Arrochar (Walk 5) after completing the circular walk described here.

Arrival at Arrochar & Tarbet Station gives you the undoubted feeling that you are in the Scottish Highlands. This destination was described in 1895 as: "[The] most individual point on the whole route, a better spot for the tourist to break his journey could not be imagined, for he is in the very heart of the picturesque", *Mountain, Moor & Loch.*

The short circular walk here follows forest tracks constructed in 1993 in a collaborative venture between the Friends of Loch Lomond and Forest Enterprise. The route passes through mixed woodland as well as conifers and the views over Loch Lomond to Ben Lomond are superb and well repay the effort of a steep ascent up the lower slopes of Cruach Tairbeirt.

*   *   *

Turn right through the underpass at the foot of the steps leading down from the station platform and follow the track which rises quite steeply to a junction where the left fork goes to Arrochar (see

Walks 5, 6 & 7). Our route goes right here to pass beside some fine old beech trees. The track undulates through some mixed woodland before turning left and ascending quite steeply upwards past some old tanks and then a pretty waterfall. (There is a right fork crossing the burn which is the route on which you will return.) As you ascend the steep path ahead, views to the rear open up with Loch Lomond and Ben Lomond standing majestically on the far bank. The burn to your right is flanked by deciduous trees and to the left of the track the plantation comprises larch, which sheds its needles in winter, and spruce. Follow the main track to swing right across a ford over the burn.

There is a slight rise as the track curves to right and then left before descending steeply to a level stretch between mature conifers. If you proceed quietly you may be fortunate and see some roe or red deer here, and there is ample evidence of their presence in the cloven hoof prints and spoor (droppings) on the ground.

Very soon the trees on the right cease and there are open views right down Loch Lomond as far as Rowardennan; the conical peak of Ben Lomond stands sentinel over the Loch while, immediately below the hillside, Tarbet nestles at the bend in the Loch where cruise boats ply from the pier. Across the rooftop of the Tarbet Hotel the busy A82 road heads southwards along the bonnie banks.

The track curves leftwards and rises gradually a short way over a grassy stretch; after crossing a small burn turn right at a T-junction. (The route to the left is a foresters' track and soon terminates.) Our route curves left and undulates along between the trees, with gaps affording further views of Loch Lomond. The conifers give way to young birch trees as the track descends to cross a burn on a substantial bridge - keep right; the left-hand track is for vehicles fording the burn. From the point where the tracks rejoin a tussocky ride leads NE and this can be followed for about 200 metres to a rocky knoll which provides a fine viewpoint of the northern slopes of Ben Lomond and northwards up the Loch, becoming increasingly narrow as the steep valley sides close in.

The route winds down beside the burn with birch and rowan trees clinging precipitously to the sides of the valley. As the descent steepens the burn tumbles down more noisily alongside and the track then follows a spur before curving right beside an old wall beyond which the railway can be glimpsed. Follow down to recross the burn on another major bridge. The route bends left to undulate above the old wall and then passes through a gap in it to descend towards the railway line. There is a curve rightwards around a distinctive hillock on the left. *This almost certainly results from glacial action many millennia ago, but may well have served as a look-out post for those monitoring the route between Arrochar and Tarbet and it still affords a good view over the "tarbet", the narrow strip of land where in the thirteenth-century King Haco's Vikings dragged their boats from Loch Long to continue their plundering down Loch Lomond and into the Clyde.*

The route is now quite close to the railway line but there are still some more taunting undulations through the birch woods before it eventually passes back through the wall and ascends some 80 metres to ford a burn and rejoin the outward track to descend towards the station. This is reached by swinging left at the track junction just beyond the beech trees, but the walk can be extended by continuing ahead towards Arrochar if wished.

5. THE COBBLER (881m), BEINN NARNAIN (926m) and A'CHROIS (849m) from ARROCHAR & TARBET

SEE MAP B p27

ROUTE REVIEW

Station:	Arrochar & Tarbet
Distance:	19km (12 miles); 1410m ascent
Grade:	Serious
Maps:	OS Landranger 56; Harveys Walker's Map of the Arrochar Alps (1:40,000)
Terrain:	mainly tracks and mountain paths, steep, wet and rocky in places; some descent over grass without paths, requiring navigation skills in poor visibility
Estate:	Argyll Forest Park
Refreshments:	Tarbet - The Black Sheep Restaurant

NB. The full route can be shortened by:

a) returning after The Cobbler reducing the distance by 2km and the ascent by 430m

b) returning after Beinn Narnain reducing the distance by 2km and the ascent by 130m

The full round of these summits makes for a strenuous day but offers the satisfaction of not only a Munro (Beinn Narnain) but also ascent of what many regard as one of Scotland's most inviting and scenic mountains, The Cobbler (Ben Arthur) which falls short of Munro status by a mere 33m (109ft). Geologically the distinctive rugged summits of Ben Arthur constitute tough intrusive diorites among quartzose mica schists but their strange shapes have given rise to folklore and adoption of the name "Cobbler". Interpretations vary but one suggests that the South Peak represents the cobbler at work bending over with his elbows extended and the North Peak is his wife Jean; Allt a'Bhalachain (Buttermilk Burn) represents milk she has spilt trickling down the hillside. The less popular A'Chrois (The Cross) is reached via a delightful ridge from Beinn Narnain. There are opportunities to shorten this walk as indicated in the Route Review above.

*   *   *

From Arrochar & Tarbet Station proceed to Arrochar; a footpath through the woods initiated by the Friends of Loch Lomond and constructed in 1993 leads from the underpass at the railway station. The track climbs quite steeply up from the underpass to a junction (where the right fork takes you on the forest walk described in 4); turn left and follow the track undulating through the woodland to reach increasingly open views of the surrounding mountains, Ben Reoch to the left and Tullich Hill (Walk 3). Your destination summits: The Cobbler, Ben Narnain (lower slopes) and A'Chrois come dramatically into sight as you approach a viewpoint overlooking the head of Loch Long where there is a choice of paths.

Our route takes the right-hand of the two newly constructed paths to descend through the birch trees into Arrochar emerging on to the A83 opposite Craigard Stores. Cross the road and turn right following the road round the head of Loch Long to the Argyll Forest Park sign (GR 294049). Take the path which leads up past a cairn (for donations to the local mountain rescue team) through the forest; this is known as the "pipe track", and follows the foundations of a cableway which was used to transport materials up the hill during the construction of water diversions to Loch Sloy Hydro Electric Power Scheme in the 1940s (see Walk 7).

After climbing steeply for about 250 metres a forest road is reached; the forest here has been cleared giving excellent views across Loch Long to Arrochar and the railway on the lower slopes of Tullich Hill. Turn left along this forest road. If forest harvesting is in progress, be sure for your own safety to observe warning signs and instructions from operators.

NB. This road may be closed for harvesting operations. If so it will be necessary to continue ahead up the pipe track following the route of Walk 6 to the Narnain Boulders, and then take the track which crosses the Allt a'Bhalachain and climbs steeply up to the col between the Centre and North Peaks of The Cobbler. Otherwise....

Continue along and then up the forest road for about 2km avoiding a track down to the left; there is much variety in the plantation, and views open up down the apparently aptly named Loch Long (*Loch Longue* means the ship loch!).

Shortly after a forest road joins from the right, our road emerges from the mature trees, and a small path comes up from Ardgarten; this continues across the forest road and our route follows it up to the right. It is somewhat indistinct, but follows a wide gap in the newly planted trees. At the top of the plantation it is tempting to head round to the left, but the best route continues towards the ridge crest ahead, still following a faint path which winds upwards.

When the ridge crest is reached the path along it is followed towards the NW for about 1¾km to the foot of the South Peak of The Cobbler. It is a mainly grassy ridge, with some undulations, and offers views across Glen Croe to The Brack and Ben Donich on the left, of the peaks of The Cobbler ahead and of Beinn Narnain on the right. As the South Peak is approached the ridge becomes steeper, and at its rocky foot the path leads round to the left, the South Peak itself being accessible only as a moderate rock climb. After crossing some large boulders, the path continues up steeply beneath the sheer west wall of the South Peak to reach the col between the South and Centre Peaks. A rocky arête leads on to the Centre Peak, which is the highest of the Cobbler summits, with an easier path beneath it on the left.

The summit block itself presents a not inconsiderable challenge to the non-rock climber and its ascent was a test of nerve for would-be chiefs of the Campbell clan. It can be ascended by passing through a "window " from the north side to reach a ledge which gives access to a subsidiary block on the east side of the main summit block, and the top of the main block is fairly readily attained from this. There are no great technical difficulties, but the ledge is exposed and the descent may prove a little more tricky, so many hill walkers will appreciate the security of a rope provided by an experienced climber, particularly if the rock is at all wet and slippery. This airy vantage point offers superb views, not least the distinctive conical summit of Ben Lomond.

From the summit proceed down NE to the col below the North Peak; this is the second col to be reached. From here the North Peak can be climbed with much less difficulty than might be expected from its massive overhangs when seen from the E or SE. A well worn path leads up rocky slabs to the cairn, keeping to the left of the overhangs which provide considerable challenges for rock climbers. On a clear day there are exceptional views from here, inevitably to Ben Lomond but also across the Rest and Be Thankful to Beinn an Lochain and northwards to Ben Ime and Ben Vane, with Ben Oss and its neighbours (Walk 10) peeping between the two.

Return to the col below the North Peak and from there proceed downhill NNW for about 100 metres to gain a path traversing the hillside and leading almost due north. After about 300 metres this path turns a little to the right and descends steeply to the very flat bealach between The Cobbler and Beinn Narnain.

NB. A descent to Loch Long (a) can be made directly from here following the path to the right which leads down to the Allt a'Bhalachain.

For Beinn Narnain turn to the left along the path, leaving it after about 100 metres to ascend the slopes of Beinn Narnain. The route is essentially E, and there is a somewhat indistinct path which can be followed, but this is easily missed. The summit of Beinn Narnain is very flat and there are a series of cairns on it in addition to a trig pillar. There are excellent views all around.

NB. A direct descent from here to Loch Long (b) can be made down the south-east ridge, over Cruach nam Miseag, to Succoth. The start of this is a steep gully on the N side of Spearhead Ridge, about 150 metres E of the trig point, and there is a path all the way down, but it is usually very wet and muddy and cannot be recommended except after a spell of dry weather.

A much more attractive option is the delightful ridge to A'Chrois, and the descent from there to Succoth, but much of this route is without paths and requires navigation skills particularly in poor visibility. For this, descend the slopes to the NE from the summit of Beinn Narnain; they are steep and boulder-strewn at first, but then become less steep and grassy. After this descent the ridge continues for about 1km, turning E to the final slope of A'Chrois; it is mainly grassy, but with a series of rocky knolls which can be traversed round or over, and views alternate between Ben Lomond, Loch Lomond with its many islands and the Luss Hills (Walk 3) to the right, and Beinn Ime, Ben Vane and Ben Vorlich (Walk 8) across the valley of the Allt Coiregrogain (Walk 6) to the left. The final ascent of A'Chrois is towards the NE. *From its cairn Loch Sloy (Walk 7) can be seen, and to the E are Inveruglas and Inversnaid on either side of Loch Lomond with Arklet Water and Loch Katrine beyond, occupying a major west-east valley thought to predate the excavation of Loch Lomond by glaciers from the north.*

To descend from A'Chrois, head back to the SW for about 400 metres, and then turn S along the side of a large knoll to find a gully leading into a small valley. A path follows this valley, providing a route down through the crags and on to the top of a ridge leading SE. This rather discontinuous and grassy ridge is followed down towards the SE, turning gradually towards the S to reach a fence round a forest plantation which has been felled and replanted. A small path leads down S alongside this fence, about 100 metres to the E of the Allt Sugach which has been dammed here to provide a water intake for Loch Sloy. This path descends steeply between the forest and the Allt Sugach, crossing two forest roads, to reach the minor road leading to the hamlet of Succoth. Turn left along this and then ahead to a telephone box from which a path leads down to the main A83 road at the head of Loch Long. You can then retrace your steps and follow the forest path from Arrochar back to the station, or alternatively continue on the pavement alongside the A83 to the station.

6. AROUND BEINN NARNAIN and A'CHROIS from ARROCHAR & TARBET

SEE MAP B p27

ROUTE REVIEW

Station:	Arrochar & Tarbet
Distance:	20km (12¹⁄₂ miles); 700m ascent
Grade:	Difficult
Maps:	OS Landranger 56; Harveys Walker's Map of the Arrochar Alps (1:40,000)
Terrain:	mainly clear paths and forest tracks but a steep descent of some 300m over rough ground
Estate:	Argyll Forest Park
Refreshments:	Tarbet - The Black Sheep Restaurant

This route offers a varied ramble through the Arrochar Alps and splendid views of the surrounding peaks which constitute this mountain group; most of the route is via paths and forest roads but there is a steep descent over rough ground from Bealach a'Mhaim into Coiregrogain. A number of watercourse diversions are seen on this walk. They feed Loch Sloy for the Sloy Hydro Electric Power Scheme, forming part of the enhanced catchment area, increased from 17 sq.km to 80 sq.km - see Walk 7 for more details.

* * *

From Arrochar & Tarbet Station follow the route described in Walk 5 to the head of Loch Long (GR 294049). As in Walk 5 take the "pipe track" climbing steeply through the forest, but for this walk continue on upwards (across the forest road) to reach a major track traversing the hillside at an altitude of about 330m. You can take the pipe track all the way up, but it is perhaps pleasanter to follow it just until it levels off somewhat (before a further steep section), and then head diagonally up left; some 25 metres after an old wooden post on the right of the pipe track take the small grassy path which follows a drainage ditch along the upper boundary of an old plantation, now felled, beneath some bluffs. Follow this up alongside a ruined fence heading towards some mature forestry plantation, still standing at the time of writing but which may soon be harvested. The path is wet in places and becomes indistinct but follow the general line of the fence (the plantation boundary) and where it ends continue ahead towards a cliff where you will join the major track traversing beneath the cliff. This deviation from the upper part of the pipe track may reward you with a colourful array of wild flowers along the route.

From whichever point it is joined follow this track, which parallels an enclosed water channel, curving to the left around the lower slopes of Beinn Narnain. There are increasingly spectacular views of the three rocky peaks of The Cobbler (Ben Arthur) as you approach the small dam on the Allt a'Bhalachain (Buttermilk Burn), where water is diverted via tunnels to Loch Sloy. A well used path continues to the NW with Buttermilk Burn on the left to reach the Narnain Boulders. *These huge rocks (presumably deposited by receding glaciers) offer shelter to many a walker and have been used as an overnight "howff" by many climbers as well as offering short climbs for the rock enthusiast. High above them on the right is the spiky outline of the Spearhead ridge of Beinn Narnain (Walk 5).*

Where the main path you have been following crosses Buttermilk Burn towards The Cobbler (the alternative route of ascent mentioned in Walk 5), turn right off this and over a boggy stretch of ground to continue with Buttermilk Burn on your left up a smaller path leading to Bealach a'Mhaim (the pass on the ridge). Shortly after a reed-filled lochan to your right the path swings right and traverses a gentle slope to meet a fence at the bealach. Cross the fence via the stile; Beinn Ime (1011m), the highest of the Arrochar Alps, lies ahead and there are long views left across the head of Glen Croe towards Ben Donich but your route lies down to the NE.

Turn right over some very marshy ground to follow the line of the fence which soon heads down very steeply on drier ground towards a distant white post and plantation served by forest roads in the Coiregrogain valley. It is steep and rough going and you may find the best line of descent to be some 15 metres from the fence down a slope with wild thrift on its ledges.

As the gradient eases near the bottom you can pick up a slight path near to the fence on your right. At a fence junction cross over a stile next to a gate in the corner and head along a grassy path on the right bank of a small burn; cross over the burn as soon as convenient to head through newly planted conifers towards an isolated telegraph pole standing near the end of a forest track you will be joining. To reach the track you need to cross a burn which emerges from underground (another diversion to Loch Sloy), near the telegraph pole; then follow the forest track downhill to a dam from which water is channelled to Loch Sloy. 50 metres beyond the dam turn sharp right down a track to cross the usually dry Allt Coiregrogain on a small causeway.

Continue upwards and then turn sharp left along the forest road heading back to Arrochar. This passes through forest plantation - if forest harvesting is in progress, be sure for your own safety to observe warning signs and instructions from operators. Some of the grassy edges alongside the road have been colonised by birch and rowan softening the aspect of the conifers, and glimpses of the full height of rugged Ben Vorlich (943m - see Walk 8) may be seen above the trees as you proceed. The forest road descends gradually, swinging rightwards beneath A'Chrois, and then rises gently to reach a gate. Continue on with cleared forest to your right; winding easily down as views left of Cruach Tairbeirt (Walk 4) become superseded by the more distant unmistakable cone of Ben Lomond. As the forest opens out there are extensive views down Loch Long and you will see the forest road stretching ahead to a junction offering a zigzag route back left to Succoth and Arrochar. This provides the gentlest gradient back to the head of Loch Long but there is a more direct route. Shortly before you emerge from the forest and immediately before a concrete bridge where the forest road crosses over the Allt Sugach tumbling down a rocky bed, turn left down a steep rough path through the conifers, following the burn on your right. At the lower forest road cross over and continue following the burn down on a similar path which brings you out at Succoth. Turn left on the road and go through the hamlet, keeping the wooden houses on your left to reach a phone box. A path leads from here back to the A83 at the head of Loch Long and the outskirts of Arrochar. From here you can retrace your steps along the outward route from Arrochar along the Cruach Tairbeirt footpath, or alternatively continue along the pavement alongside the A83 to the station.

7. ARROCHAR & TARBET to ARDLUI via GLEN LOIN and LOCH SLOY

| SEE MAP B p27 |

ROUTE REVIEW

Stations:	Arrochar & Tarbet, Ardlui
Distance:	19km (12 miles); 410m ascent
Grade:	Difficult
Maps:	OS Landranger 56; Harveys Walker's Map of the Arrochar Alps (1:40,000)
Terrain:	a mixture - tracks, paths and rough ground, wet in places, and a traverse of a steep slope alongside Loch Sloy
Estates:	Argyll Forest Park; Inveruglas*; Sloy; Stuckendroin* (* see Appendix B)
Refreshments:	Ardlui Hotel; Bothan Loch Laomainn

NB. No Dogs please and keep well clear of sheep during the lambing season, April and May

Glen Loin offers a pretty route into the midst of the "Arrochar Alps". The old county boundary follows Loin Water towards Coiregrogain where a private road leads on to remote Loch Sloy, ancient gathering place of the Clan MacFarlane. The Gaelic "sloidh" means gathering or meeting place; "Loch Sloy" was the war cry of the Clan MacFarlane who for over 500 years prior to 1874 held sway in the remote terrain surrounding the once small loch. Notorious men they were and infamous cattle raiders, setting upon those passing through their lands.

Today the walker alongside Loch Sloy will encounter a very different ambience. The loch has been much enlarged: doubled in length and with its surface raised by 47m by the construction of a dam - 56m high and 357 metres long - in 1946 to provide hydro-electricity to Clydeside and Central Scotland. By diverting watercourses via aqueducts and tunnels the catchment area has been increased from 17 sq.km to 80 sq.km such that 25mm (1 inch) of rain over the catchment area will yield about 1 million units of electricity. From Loch Sloy the water is carried some 3km via a tunnel through Ben Vorlich and then by four pipelines down to the

43

power station at Inveruglas Bay on Loch Lomond. This 130 MW station began to generate electricity in 1950 and is still the largest conventional hydro-electric development in the UK.

From the dam Loch Sloy is followed northwards towards lonely Strath Dhub-uisage. The route passes through very contrasting landscape and part of this walk can be very wet.

*   *   *

From Arrochar & Tarbet Station Glen Loin is reached by following the forest footpath described in the first paragraph of Walk 5 as far as the viewpoint overlooking the head of Loch Long where there is a choice of paths. On the left near the viewpoint you will see a concrete post and water inspection cover. On the right opposite these a small grassy level path leads off traversing along the hillside. Leave the newly constructed path and follow this grassy path between the gorse and shrubs - it takes the route along a water supply coming down from Loch Sloy and you will see small white posts saying "water"; it is wet underfoot!

After passing under some wires the path descends gradually into mixed woodland and widens out into a stony track beneath the trees. It emerges on to a farm track at Stronafyne farm just beyond some sheep pens. Turn right on the farm track through a gateway and follow it between a field on your left and a fence to your right. After passing a corrugated barn and fording a small stream which flows across the track, you reach another gateway. Continue through along a leafy lane flanked by rowans and silver birches with wild meadow flowers in more open grassy parts.

After about 2km proceed through a further gate onto open land where a path can be seen roughly following the line of the pylons stretching ahead of you. Take the path, which is wet in places and meanders a little, first to the right and then to the left of the direct route of the pylon line. *The path passes a remarkably adaptable holly tree whose main trunk, having fallen to the ground some time ago, now supports vigorous branches at right angles growing upwards, heavily berried in winter. As you climb gently upwards between the oak woodland to your right and the conifers to your left take a last look back at Loch Long.*

A gentle ascent of 1km takes you to a col from which the path drops down a short way and becomes less distinct. Keeping ahead towards Ben Vorlich and following the general line of the pylons, pick your way across a flatter stretch which is rather boggy in places. A short climb takes you to a small hill topped by a pylon, a vantage point from which to see not only Ben Vorlich ahead (with the upper station of the Sloy Hydroelectric scheme now visible low on its right-hand flank) but also Ben Lomond to the south-east and Ben Vane to the north-west peeping over the near hill (Dubh Chnoc).

Continue N over the rather wet grassland until in about $^3/_4$km a ride opens up (half left) in the forestry plantation. Follow this route between the conifers to a fence which you cross and then turn right down to a bridge over Inveruglas Water. A short track from this bridge leads up to the private Hydro Electric road to Loch Sloy. Turn left along this; in about $^1/_2$km you will pass a gravel road over a bridge heading up the valley towards Beinn Ime (1011m), the highest of the Arrochar Alps.

Keep ahead towards the Sloy Dam on the tarmac road which follows the tumbling river descending from Sloy. On reaching the dam climb steeply up on the right to the top. A right of way along an ancient drove road used to follow the shoreline of Loch Sloy but was flooded when the level was raised by the hydroelectric scheme so the onward route is now more difficult. From the top of the dam follow a small (sheep) track along the steep slope above Loch Sloy; this requires surefootedness and where there have been occasional small land slips extra care is needed. After the first $^1/_2$km the slope becomes less severe. Continue along the shore of Loch Sloy to a peninsula which juts out; from here strike diagonally up and round the slope towards the pylons on your right.

There are two alternative routes to Ardlui from here. The more straightforward a) crosses to the N side of Strath Dubh-uisage but involves a walk of $1^1/_4$km along the busy A82 road and at the time of writing there is no pavement or footpath alongside the road (see Walk 10). Alternative b) avoids this walk along the road.

Alternative a): go downwards to the right of the pylons in a straightish line towards the outlet of an aqueduct which can then be followed, along the side of a plantation to a gate. Turn right on a track, then almost immediately left along the aqueduct, across the dam and over a stile alongside a gate into a new plantation. Continue following the aqueduct; it makes a good raised track! Where it ends at a dam, head diagonally down through the plantation to the line of pylons which are followed and then pick a route above a fence heading right through Strath Dhub-uisage. When the ground begins to fall away steeply head down towards a pylon. From here a red sign on a railway bridge over the West Highland line becomes visible - continue down to this. Cross the railway and continue ahead and right to a stile at the side of the A82. Turn right along the road taking care and walking to face the oncoming traffic to Ardlui Station.

Alternative b): to avoid the road walk, keep on the S side of Strath Dubh-uisage, following an aqueduct to the NW which carries water from the northern slopes of Ben Vorlich to Loch Sloy. This terminates at a small dam (GR 299156). From here head E climbing gradually to a col to the S of Stob an Fhithich. Just over this col the path from Ardlui to Ben Vorlich (Walk 8) is reached and this is followed down to Ardlui. The path first leads N round the head of a small corrie and then turns ESE to descend towards Ardlui with a burn on the right. It crosses the burn and continues past Garristuck and through a railway underpass to reach the A82 about 150 metres S of Ardlui station.

8. ARDLUI to ARROCHAR & TARBET over BEN VORLICH (943m) and via GLEN LOIN

SEE MAP B p27

ROUTE REVIEW

Stations:	Ardlui, Arrochar & Tarbet
Distance:	16km (10 miles); 1110m ascent
Grade:	Serious
Maps:	OS Landranger 56; Harveys Walker's Map of The Arrochar Alps (1:40,000)
Terrain:	rugged, steep and little path on Ben Vorlich
Estates:	Inveruglas*; Sloy; Stuckendroin*; Argyll Forest Park (* - see Appendix B)
Refreshments:	Tarbet - The Black Sheep Restaurant

NB. There are two alternatives for this walk, both returning to Ardlui:
   a) from the summit of Ben Vorlich retracing the route of ascent reducing the distance to 11km, 1020m ascent
   b) from the Sloy Dam returning to Ardlui alongside Loch Sloy (see Walk 7), increasing the distance to 18km, 1100m ascent

Ardlui Station, affording a dual track passing place for trains, is the starting point for an ascent of rugged Ben Vorlich (hill of the bay), the northern most of the Arrochar Alps. A product of Caledonian overfolding, the mountain comprises essentially a crescent-shaped ridge extending from Stob an Fhithich above Ardlui in the north towards Inveruglas in the south. It towers over the northern section of Loch Lomond and behind it lurk the dark secrets of Loch Sloy (see Walk 7). Ardlui Hotel, opposite the station, some 150 years old, used to be a Colquhoun hunting lodge and is reputedly haunted by a ghostly apparition clad in eighteenth-century dress.

*   *   *

Turn right out of the station and walk about 150 metres S on the A82 to take the private road under the railway passing "Garristuck" and a new cottage on the left. Go through a gate and head WNW along the path; do not cross the burn on your left but cross the burn ahead and continue up the path (which passes through bracken in summer) with this second burn on your left. As you approach Stob an Fhithich (419m) swing left beneath some rocky knolls to reach the ridge just S of Stob an Fhithich. After a short descent climb the broad ridge of Stob nan Coinnich Bhacain heading SSW and then due S past a small lochan. From the top turn SW and descend about 80m to an elongated col. (There are escape routes back to Ardlui from here should bad weather set in down the E side from the SW end of the col, or down the NW side from anywhere along the col.)

From the col continue SW up the ridge ahead which is steep and rocky on the left so keep to the right. After about 1km the ridge swings left towards the SSE and becomes smoother in character rather than rocky or hummocky, and shortly the cairn on the N summit (931m) is reached. From here head just E of S for 1/2km, down and then up, to the main summit (943m) of Ben Vorlich and on some 150 metres to a trig point (941m) from which there are excellent views down Loch Lomond.

Alternative a): from here the shortest return to Ardlui is by retracing the steps of your ascent.

The continuation of the walk involves a steep descent to the Hydro Electric road from Inveruglas to Sloy Dam. First, however, it is necessary to continue along the main ridge of Ben Vorlich for about 1¹/₄km, but it is preferable initially to head SW for about 100 metres to reach what may be best described as an "open valley" just below the ridge. This is followed to the SSE; after about 600 metres Sloy Dam can be seen below and there is a steep way down to it (used in the Arrochar Alps Hill Race), but it is easier to continue SSE for a further 600 metres to the head of a corrie which offers a better line of descent. It is easiest to the left of the corrie and this steep descent will take you down to the Hydro Electric road which was followed in Walk 7.

Alternative b): from here follow the latter part of Walk 7 alongside Loch Sloy back to Ardlui Station - see Walk 7 for details.

The continuation of the walk to Arrochar & Tarbet Station reverses the earlier part of Walk 7 through Glen Loin; turn left along the Sloy Dam road and follow this downhill, continuing past the first right turn which crosses the river descending from Loch Sloy. About ¹/₂km beyond this junction turn right down a track to a bridge across Inveruglas Water. Turn up to the left and shortly cross a fence beyond which is a forestry plantation. Follow along a "ride" between the conifers to emerge at the far side of the plantation where a line of pylons runs southwards across rather wet grassland. Turn right and follow the general line of the pylons picking your way through the boggier parts; there is a path, somewhat indistinct in parts and meandering, but roughly following the direction taken by the pylons. Eventually you pass through a gate from the open land onto a farm track.

As you approach Stronafyne Farm go through a gate and then, immediately before a sheep pen and low barn to the left of the farm track, turn to the left to join a stony wet track leading upwards beneath the trees, following the line of a water supply route coming from Loch Sloy. As more open ground is reached the track levels off and you will shortly reach a viewpoint and join the network of paths on the lower slopes of Cruach Tairbeirt initiated by the Friends of Loch Lomond. From the viewpoint take the track heading around the hillside eastwards towards Tarbet, Loch Lomond and the station; at a junction the right-hand track descends to the station.

9. ARDLUI TO CRIANLARICH via BEN GLAS WATERFALL and GLEN FALLOCH

> SEE MAP C p50

ROUTE REVIEW

Stations:	**Ardlui, Crianlarich**
Distance:	**15km (9½ miles); 490m ascent**
Grade:	**Moderate**
Map:	**OS Landranger 50**
Terrain:	**mainly on fairly level West Highland Way but diversion up alongside Ben Glas Burn involves a steep path, needing care**
Ferry:	**Ardlui to Ardleish (tel. 03014 243 or 03014 244)**
Estate:	**Glenfalloch (see Appendix B)**
Refreshments:	**Crianlarich - Station Tearoom**
	Inverarnan (slightly off route) - Drovers Inn; Stagger Inn

This walk features two waterfalls and you will be following historic routes through Glen Falloch established by eighteenth-century drovers and soldiers, now incorporated into the West Highland Way, a long distance footpath from the outskirts of Glasgow to Fort William, a distance of some 152km (95 miles). The first long-distance footpath in Scotland, it was opened in 1980 and takes the walker from the lowlands to the highlands through very varied scenery from picturesque Loch Lomondside, which nevertheless offers a strenuous challenge, to remote and rugged Rannoch Moor and thence to the foot of Britain's highest mountain, Ben Nevis.

The military road, which it follows for much of its way, was built in 1752 and 1753 being part of a network established in the Scottish Highlands by Major Caulfield, successor to General Wade, as a means for handling Jacobite uprisings. This glen also provides the route for the railway. In 1845, the area saw a dispute between the Caledonian Northern Direct line and the Scottish Grand Junction

49

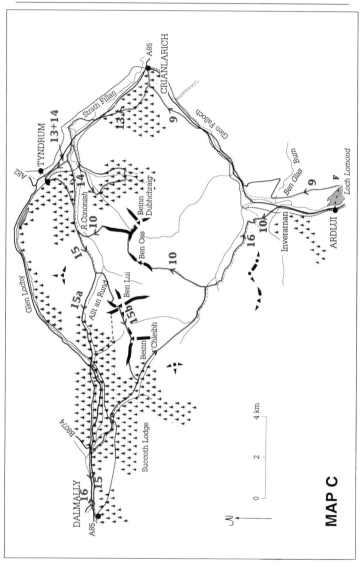

MAP C

0   2   4 km

N

regarding various proposed routes for a railway through the Glen. The former were deemed to have trespassed into Glen Falloch, the property of the Marquis of Breadalbane whose men overthrew them. It was to be another forty-five years before the present railway route passed through Glen Falloch.

Our route also involves a ferry crossing of Loch Lomond and a climb alongside the fine waterfall of Ben Glas Burn to reach the edge of an area which, considering its proximity to the busy A82, feels surprisingly remote - the drumlins and boulder-strewn landscape before you, foothills to the trackless mountains beyond, seem to belong to another planet. There may seem little evidence of man's impact here but the once forested landscape has been denuded by felling, burning and grazing. A few remnants of the ancient Caledonian pine forest will be seen as the West Highland Way is followed up Glen Falloch.

In preglacial times the drainage of this area was thought to be towards the E or NE into the Tay and Forth; however glaciers travelling southwards scoured out a glacial "trench" now occupied by Loch Lomond and the River Falloch which is fed by the watercourses of adjacent hanging valleys, legacies of the earlier drainage pattern.

In winter, when the ferry is not operating across Loch Lomond, the A82 can be followed (with care, if no footpath has yet been provided, as it is a busy road) from Ardlui to Inverarnan (see Walk 10) and the route joined at Beinglas Farm.

*   *   *

From Ardlui Station cross the A82 to the Ardlui Hotel and then take the small, privately-run ferry across the Loch. (It runs only during the summer months.) The ferry will drop you off at Ardleish and from there you follow the West Highland Way along Loch Lomondside. Heading N the Way rises uphill past the old Ardleish farm to a marshy col. There is an excellent view southwards down the Loch from here and better still from the rocky knoll to the left of the path before it reaches Dubh Lochan (the black loch). Northwards lies the impressive group of peaks: Beinn Dubhchraig, Ben Oss and Ben Lui (see Walks 10 & 15) across Glen Falloch.

Continue along the Way through the woods where you might be

fortunate enough to see the feral goats which frequent this area. *Legend has it that Robert the Bruce, as a fugitive, once shared a cave along the east shore of Loch Lomond with the goats for warmth - so grateful was he that he passed a law protecting them.*

You pass beneath the power lines leading to and from Cruachan Power Station on Loch Awe (see Walk 21) before reaching the footbridge across Ben Glas burn which has cascaded down a series of waterfalls to reach this point.

From here those with time and inclination for a detour can sidetrack to sample the historic Drover's Inn set in rather a timewarp at Inverarnan. *The Inn has had a colourful history: as the name implies it was a droving inn as far back as the early 1700s - in the days when drovers took their beasts down Loch Lomondside to the cattle fairs at Crieff and Falkirk. In the nineteenth century the Inn was a popular destination for steamboats which plied from the Loch up the River Falloch which was canalised to take them. At the end of the century the Inn was used as a residence for engineers working on the West Highland Railway. Between the two periods it was for a time a temperance hotel but the thirsty walker of today can rest assured that this is no longer the case. Across the road the Stagger Inn, named after a local fishing pool and in sympathy with footsore walkers, offers "the taste of the glens".* To reach Inverarnan turn left and follow the bank of the burn to cross the River Falloch over the bridge leading to Beinglas Farm and then walk carefully along the A82 for about 250 metres. Equally carefully(!) retrace your steps to rejoin the route at the bridge over the Ben Glas burn.

From the footbridge continue N, signposted Crianlarich, for some 50 metres and cross a stile. Now, leaving the West Highland Way, take the path up the hillside behind Beinglas Farm. On meeting a fence continue along the path to the left to a stile over it, and then proceed diagonally up the hillside to the right to approach Ben Glas Burn where it descends in spectacular waterfalls. The path zigzags fairly steeply up the hill with the burn on the right. As you reach more level ground (around a major curve in the burn) a track can be seen leading off to the left.

NB. It is possible to extend the walk from this point by following the N side of the burn as it winds between drumlins for some $2^{1/2}$km to reach Lochan Beinn Chabhair, a beautiful remote lochan lying beneath Beinn Chabhair (931 metres) ahead. (From here the more intrepid and energetic can climb up to the ridge on the left to the summit of Beinn Chabhair.) To return, retrace your route back to the track identified above.

This stony double track to the left, perhaps an old drove road, leads N, ascending slightly for a short distance before wending its way gently downhill. Looking across Glen Falloch you see the West Highland Railway line crossing a major viaduct - its centre span only 2m less in height than the Forth Railway Bridge - over Dhub Eas (black water) opposite. Continue on downhill as the path zigzags more steeply to meet the West Highland Way, a wide gravel track at this point. Turn right and follow the Way N.

As the Way ascends the Glen, the River Falloch tumbles down over wide ledges and through rocky gorges, the most spectacular of which is at the Falls of Falloch, reached just over 1km from the point where you rejoined the West Highland Way. You will see a burn (Allt Fionn Ghlinne) descending on the far side to meet the Falloch; after this the Way crosses a footbridge and rises for some 50 metres to cross another footbridge. The Falls are on the left some 200 metres beyond this second footbridge; they are screened by tree foliage in summer and there are steep slopes into the river, so take care. *The pool beneath the falls is known as Rob Roy's bath tub in connection with legendary ablutions of this local hero. Beyond the Falls on the north-west side of the Glen is the huge boulder of Clach-na-Briton (the "stone of the Britons") which supposedly designated the boundaries of the Britons, the Scots and the Picts. The boulder formed the boundary stone between the ancient Kingdoms of Pictland, Dalriada and Strathclyde. Legend has it that Robert the Bruce stopped here to ensure he was not being followed after his defeat at Dalrigh (see Walk 13).*

The Way continues to follow the SE side of the river to Derrydaroch (the oak grove) where it crosses over the river and between some isolated remnants of Caledonian pines. Passing under the railway and then over the A82 road the Way rises uphill to follow the line of an old military road to Crianlarich. Traversing the hillside the old road affords open views of the fine peaks to the right as you approach Crianlarich: Cruach Ardrain (1045m - see Walk 12) and conical Ben More (1174m). When you reach a stile in a deer fence the West Highland Way continues on leftwards to Tyndrum (Walk 13) but Crianlarich is reached by turning right at this point and taking a winding path through young conifers over a spur which leads down shortly to the A82 almost opposite the entrance to Crianlarich station.

10. ARDLUI to TYNDRUM over BEN OSS (1028m)

SEE MAP C p50

ROUTE REVIEW

Stations:	**Ardlui, Lower Tyndrum**
Distance:	**22km (13¹/₂ miles); 1260m ascent**
Grade:	**Serious**
Map:	**OS Landranger 50**
Terrain:	**the mountain terrain is mainly heather or grass, though there are some rocky sections; the approach and final 4km are on vehicle tracks**
Estates:	**Glenfalloch*; Cononish Farm; Forest Enterprise (Lorne District) (* see Appendix B)**
Refreshments:	**Inverarnan - Drovers Inn; Stagger Inn**
	Tyndrum - West Highlander Restaurant; Little Chef

The remote location of Ben Oss (loch-outlet hill) and its neighbour Beinn Dubhchraig (black rock hill) between Glen Falloch and Strath Fillan makes an approach from Ardlui and return to Tyndrum particularly appropriate. From near Ardlui Ben Oss presents a pleasing profile, a distinctive cone, while Beinn Dubhchraig reveals a craggy aspect.

The descent to the Cononish glen overlooks an area where recent prospecting for gold has led to plans for commercial gold mining with approval by the local district council despite concerns regarding pollution of the Tay river system and visual impact in an unspoilt mountain area. The plans involve blasting caverns about 250m down with the potential of some ninety jobs!

*   *   *

From Ardlui Station proceed N alongside the A82 for 3km to Inverarnan; at the time of writing the possibility of a footpath between Ardlui and Inverarnan was being pursued by the Loch

Lomond Park Authority and others, and hopefully by the time you are reading this there will be a footpath available for you to use. If not take great care walking along this busy main road. As you approach Inverarnan there are good views of Beinn Glas waterfall to the right (see Walk 9). At Inverarnan turn left immediately before the Stagger Inn, alongside the keeper's cottage following a lane to pass beneath the railway. From here head uphill to follow below the line of pylons for about ³/₄km to join a vehicle track which is zigzagging uphill. Turn left up this track and shortly at a T-junction turn right to follow the track which climbs a little higher and then traverses the hillside above Gleann nan Caorann alongside a conduit with a series of intakes, carrying water destined for the Loch Sloy Hydro Electric Scheme (see Walk 7). After about 3¹/₂km a pipeline crosses the valley bringing water from the opposite side and a track leads down to follow it; take this track and at the N end of the pipeline turn right, still on a vehicle track to cross the bed of the Allt nan Caorainn below the water intake from it.

This track climbs steadily for about 1¹/₂km over peaty terrain. At its end continue in the same direction over rough ground with a burn on the left. The burn becomes incised higher up and our route remains above it on the right, climbing fairly steeply at one stage and heading N. After the ground has levelled off considerably, a broad ridge is reached rising from the col between Ben Lui and Ben Oss, and if it is clear, Ben Lui is seen to the NW; the steep rocky slope to the NNE leads to the summit of Ben Oss marked by a large cairn.

From the summit a fairly easy ridge leads onwards to the NNE, curving to the right as a substantial knoll is reached. Beinn Dubhchraig is seen to the right with the ridge leading round to it, and below on the left can be seen Cononish Farm and the gold mine workings by the Eas Anie. Beyond the knoll the route turns E and the ground becomes more broken down to a col above Loch Oss on the right with more of Loch Lomond coming into view in the distance beyond. The descent northwards from this col is steep and not recommended; it is better to follow the path which zigzags up the steep slope ahead to gain the shoulder of Beinn Dhubchraig. Here, when the gradient has eased, some interconnected lochans will be reached which indicate the descent route. However, the summit of Beinn Dubhchraig is only a further ¹/₂km to the SE with an ascent of about 75m so, unless time is short, this Munro - giving excellent views down Loch Lomond and of the hills across Strath Fillan and Glen Falloch - can well be included in the day, returning to these lochans for the descent.

From the lochans head N down a broad and easy ridge. After 1km or so the ridge curves to the right and the gradient decreases, but the northern end of the ridge has been truncated (by the ice which once flowed down the valley from Ben Lui) and care must be taken in descending it. A modern fence with wooden posts will be met running across the end of the ridge; this is followed downhill to the left to a corner with a gate (GR 307278). Pass through the gate and continue down the grassy slope with the gradient becoming steeper, heading a little to the left of Cononish Farm below, to avoid the rocky ground to the right. There is a bridge across the River Cononish SE of the farm and beyond this follow the farm track to the right for a little over 1km where a forest road to the left is taken leading in just over 2km to Tyndrum Lower Station.

11. AN CAISTEAL (995m) and BEINN a'CHROIN (940m) from CRIANLARICH

SEE MAP D p58

ROUTE REVIEW

Station:	Crianlarich
Distance:	18km (11 miles); 990m ascent
Grade:	Serious
Map:	OS Landranger 50
Terrain:	some fairly steep and rocky sections with some easier ridges
Estate:	Glenfalloch (see Appendix B)
Refreshments:	Crianlarich - Station Tearoom

An Caisteal (the castle) and Beinn a'Chroin (hill of danger) overlook the headwaters of the River Falloch, above the sharp bend in this river which is attributed to changes in the drainage pattern resulting from glacial erosion and the damming of valleys by ice towards the end of the last Ice Age. On their lower slopes in Glen Falloch the isolated and often gaunt trees scattered over the moorland are Caledonian pines, remnants of extensive prehistoric forestation which was cleared some 6,000 years ago as man began to provide pasture for animals. The grazing inhibited regeneration of seedling trees but an area nearby is fenced to encourage the growth of new pines.

These mountains provide excellent routes for the hill-walker, with some delightful ridges, and are readily accessible from Crianlarich Station, though this does involve a walk of 2km along the A82 at the beginning and end of the day.

* * *

From Crianlarich Station proceed for about 2km SW along the A82. When the plantation at the other side of the railway comes to an end, and at the start of a stretch of old road where cars park, a track leads down through an underpass beneath the railway to a bridge over the River Falloch. Cross the bridge and continue along the track for 1¼km, passing a sheepfold on the left, to a gate in a fence. From here head SSW up the slope on the right to gain the ridge leading NNW from the summit of Sron Gharbh; a burn to the right can usefully be followed during part of this ascent.

From the top of Sron Gharbh (708m) the going is much easier along a ridge which undulates before climbing more steadily along what is known as Twistin Hill. As the top of An Caisteal is approached there are some interesting rock features which must result from the intense metamorphic processes (involving heat and pressure) which occurred when these Caledonian mountains were being formed around 500 million years ago; in particular a pronounced cleft is crossed about 150 metres before reaching a cairn on a rocky knoll which is perhaps the "castle" which gives the mountain its name. The summit is a further 200 metres beyond.

The route on to Beinn a'Chroin is to the SSW for about 100 metres and then down the ridge leading S and SSE to a level bealach (col); this ridge is steep in places, but a path finds the best way through the rocky outcrops. The west face of Beinn a'Chroin is somewhat intimidating. There is a faint path, however, which goes to the left under a small overhanging crag and then right onto the top of it; a traverse left beneath crags can be followed by an ascending traverse

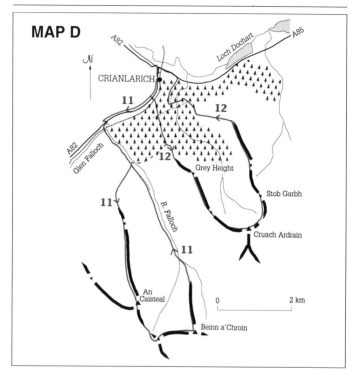

right beneath the upper line of crags. The path is now much more obvious and curves round to head NE and gain the summit ridge of Beinn a'Chroin which is about 1km long. There are extensive views of Ben Lomond to the south, with Loch Katrine, Ben Venue and the Trossachs to the south-east.

The ridge is traversed, passing two cairns on the west top and a bealach about 60m lower, before the cairn marking the higher east top is reached. The descent from Beinn a'Chroin is by the north ridge; to reach this head NNW for about 200 metres and then follow the ridge, which is steep and craggy in places, keeping near to its crest right down to the burn at its foot. This delightful burn is followed to its junction with the River Falloch, and the route is then down Coire Earb on the west side of the River Falloch. The ground is somewhat boggy, but after about 2km the track is reached which leads in a further 2km to the railway underpass and on to the A82. From here retrace your steps to the station.

12. CRUACH ARDRAIN (1045m) from CRIANLARICH

SEE MAP D p58

ROUTE REVIEW

Station:	Crianlarich
Distance:	12km (7½ miles); 1050m ascent
Grade:	Serious
Maps:	OS Landranger 50 & 51
Terrain:	steep and rocky in parts, needing care with navigation in poor visibility. The particularly steep descent from Cruach Ardrain to reach Stob Garbh can be avoided by retracing the route of ascent
Estate:	Forest Enterprise (Lorne District)
Refreshments:	Crianlarich - Station Tearoom

Cruach Ardrain (the stack of the high part), sits majestically to the SSE of Crianlarich Station, its pointed summit surmounting an impressive north face, in which is set a Y-shaped gully which offers good winter snow climbing. The mountain itself forms part of a Y with three prominent ridges extending from its summit: NW to Grey Height, (the approach described here), and NE to Stob Garbh (960m) - these enclosing Coire Ardrain; the long leg of the Y is to the SSE culminating in Beinn Tulichean.

Cruach Ardrain also forms a watershed for three distinct drainage systems - northwards tributaries flow towards the Dochart system flowing east into the Tay and thence to the North Sea; westwards the streams join the River Falloch flowing into Loch Lomond and outwards to the Clyde; south-eastwards watercourses form the River Larig flowing east into Loch Voil, then southwards through Strathyre to enter the River Teith and so via the Forth to the North Sea.

We describe here the traverse of the complete horseshoe above Coire Ardrain starting with Grey Height. The most direct route to

Grey Height involves a muddy ascent through forest; we offer an alternative (though this involves a 2km walk along the A82).

* * *

For the direct route to Grey Height proceed S from the station along the A82 for about ¹/₂km to a gate on the left opposite a house, Strona Old House. A stile by the gate leads to a bridge over the railway line; beyond this keep half right following a path to the corner of open land where a ride leads left. In about 200 metres an old fence is reached; turn right and follow the line of this uphill through the forest, crossing areas where the trees have been felled and also two recently constructed forest roads. The fence posts continue for about 1km and this part of the route can be very muddy, particularly after wet weather. When the edge of the forest can be seen on the right leave the fence posts and follow the forest edge to the top, continuing ahead to a fence. An Caisteal and then Beinn a'Chroin come into view on the right (see Walk 11), and behind there are excellent views across Glen Falloch and Strath Fillan to the hills beyond.

To avoid the often muddy ascent through the forest it is possible to follow the A82 for about 2km from the station to the end of the forest plantation on the left. Here take the track down to the underpass beneath the railway and over the bridge across the River Falloch and continue along this track leading SE (also the start of Walk 11). After about 1¹/₄km fork left down a track to a bridge back over the River Falloch, and then climb the slope ahead following the fence along the southern edge of the plantation.

Follow the fence eastwards to its highest point where Ben More comes into view, and from here head SE to ascend Grey Height (685m); this is the first summit of the horseshoe and provides a vantage point for a preview of the route ahead. Continue along the broad and pleasant ridge ahead to Meall Dhamh (814m) (an ideal point from which to view almost the entire length of Walk 11). From here there is a descent of about 50m, in two fairly steep steps following a well-established path, before the final climb up the western shoulder of Cruach Ardrain which is steep in parts. This mountain has twin peaks about 150 metres apart, each with a cairn, but that to the NE is the higher. *It offers magnificnt views in all directions: to the S is a connecting ridge to Beinn Tulaichean with the valley of the River Larig beyond and Loch Katrine beyond again; Crianlarich is seen to the NW with Strath Fillan and Tyndrum beyond and the mountains on either side, whilst Ben More and Stob Binnein dominate the view to the NE.*

The easiest way back to Crianlarich is to retrace the route of ascent. For those wishing to complete the horseshoe it is necessary to descend to the col between Cruach Ardrain and Stob Garbh; this descent is very steep and rocky, and loose in parts, and if conditions are at all difficult or any member of the party is not confident on such steep ground it should not be attempted. From the col continue northwards ascending the rocky hump of Stob Garbh (the rough peak).

Beyond this top there is steepish descent to the NW, continuing along an easy grassy ridge N over Stob Coire Bhuidhe and a further knoll to a fence, about 2km beyond the summit of Stob Garbh. There are various possible ways through the forest to Crianlarich. For the route we have chosen to describe here, follow the fence down to the left (WNW) to a fence junction, and continue down in the same general direction, but heading increasingly to the right to remain a little above the forest but below the crags on Creag na h-Iolaire. About 3/4km beyond the fence junction a wide grassy ride will be seen leading down into the forest towards NNW (directly towards Crianlarich below). Proceed down this ride and when it meets another ride continue in the same direction through the trees to a grassy path which leads on down eventually to reach a new forest road. This provides the easiest (though not the shortest) way back to Crianlarich. Turn left along this which leads in about 1/2km to another forest road; a sharp right turn here leads under the overhead power lines to the A85 road at the eastern end of Crianlarich. Turn left along here to return to the station.

INTRODUCTION

At Crianlarich the West Highland Railway used to cross over the Caledonian Callandar to Oban Line which had been finally completed in 1880, before which time a railhead had been established at Tyndrum. Despite early pressure for a link to provide a direct passenger service between Glasgow and Oban this was not effected until 1949 (though there had been some earlier special excursion trains). Subsequently, in 1965, the line between Callander and Crianlarich was closed; it was already scheduled for closure when a rockfall across the line in Glen Ogle precipitated its demise. The remaining section to Oban is now fully integrated with the West Highland Line at Crianlarich, and the two are incorporated into a jointly timetabled service.

The Oban branch follows Strath Fillan, looping into Cononish Glen which gives access to our walks in the Ben Lui area, including the ascent of that fine mountain. The Line follows Glen Lochy to Dalmally and Loch Awe from which mighty Ben Cruachan and its neighbouring peaks can be explored. At Taynuilt it reaches fiord-like Loch Etive before going on to somewhat gentler terrain and the pretty sea port at Oban, all with their own particular interest, which we explore in Walks 23 to 26.

13. CRIANLARICH TO TYNDRUM via ANCIENT PINE FOREST

SEE MAP C p50

ROUTE REVIEW

Stations:	Crianlarich, Tyndrum Lower
Distance:	20km (12½ miles); 430m ascent
Grade:	Moderate
Map:	OS Landranger 50
Terrain:	good clear path along the West Highland Way; the path climbing through the ancient forest may be wet and there

is a burn to be crossed
Estates: **Forest Enterprise (Lorne District); Auchreoch; Strathfillan**
Refreshments: **Tyndrum - West Highlander Restaurant; Little Chef**

NB. The walk into the pine forest can be undertaken as a circular route from Tyndrum Station and the distance will be reduced to 15km.

The simple route from Crianlarich to Tyndrum is to follow the waymarked (by thistle markers) path of the West Highland Way. (Note that the access agreement with a proprietor here explicitly forbids dogs.) This route leads past St Fillans Priory which has many legendary traditions associated with it. St Fillan was an Irish monk and missionary in the area during the eighth century and there are relics of his - a crozier and a bell - in the National Museum of Antiquities in Edinburgh. Adjacent to the Priory was a Holy Pool where the sick seeking healing were dipped. Lunatics however were bound and thrown in; in the unlikely event that they could bring up a pebble from the bottom they were declared cured and the pebble was added to a cairn on the bank.

We have included a diversion from the Way through the remnants of ancient Caledonian Pine Forest in Coille Coire Chuilc, in which efforts are being made to promote regeneration; please "tread gently" here to minimise impact. It provides a stiking contrast with much more recent forestry plantations. The diversion involves an extension towards Beinn Dubhchraig and a climb to about 450m below the mountain, before returning through Gleann Auchreoch to pick up the West Highland Way again.

* * *

Leave the station via the underpass and turn S for a few metres along the A82, then cross over to pick up the spur leading onto (and signed to) the West Highland Way. The path winds up a tree-clad shoulder and as you gain height it is worth looking back at the superb views across the station towards Cruach Ardrain (Walk 12) and its neighbours. The path drops down slightly to join the Way as it comes over a stile from its ascent up Glen Falloch. Head right in a westerly direction towards Tyndrum through some forestry plantation. The Way turns northwards and descends, crossing the

Herive Burn, towards the railway and A82 at Ewich. Pass under the railway and continue between the line and the A82 to the point where the road is crossed and then join the farm track which leads across the River Fillan, skirting the remains of St Fillans Priory.

Continue along the Way past Auchtertyre Farm and down to re-cross the A82, following the river bank to the old White Bridge at GR 345288. The Way continues onwards to Tyndrum and this route is picked up again later but the Pine Forest extension is now described.

Cross the bridge over the River Fillan and turn right on the rough track heading W alongside the railway line. In 1km cross the railway by a bridge and almost at once leave the track and follow a path to the right alongside the railway to a footbridge over the Allt Gleann Auchreoch. Cross the bridge and turn left following the path alongside the Allt Gleann Auchreoch and its tributary, the Allt Coire Dubhchraig. Here the path winds its way amongst the ancient pines of the Coille Coire Chuilc. The burn on your left flows down a small gorge and tumbles down a waterfall.

With splendid views of Beinn Dubhchraig opening up all the while, the path leads you onwards to a stile over a high deer fence; keep fairly near to the burn, crossing small tributaries, and you will then encounter another stile over a second high fence beyond which there has been new forestry planting. After a distance of a further $^{1}/_{2}$km from the second stile and above a series of waterfalls, you will see a forest road terminating about 150 metres from the burn on the other side of it. (This is about 200 metres before you would reach a fence along the topside of the plantation.) To make this part of your walk into a round trip it is necessary to cross the burn here so as to reach the forest road beyond it. (Should you find the burn to be uncrossable you will need to retrace your steps.) Alternatively if any in your party are Munro-baggers they can continue ahead for the ascent of Beinn Dubhchraig and descend by the route described in Walk 10.

However unless the burn is in spate you should have no difficulty crossing it to join the forest road which leads E, zigzags downhill, and then follows the contours southwards on the W side of Gleann Auchreoch before it descends to a bridge over the Allt Gleann Auchreoch. After the bridge there is a short ascent to a junction with a forest road following the E side of Gleann Auchreoch. Turn left

Dalmally Horseshoe (18)
Kilchurn Castle (19)

To Dunollie (25) across Oban Bay from Pulpit Hill (26)
Across Loch Tulla (26 & 31)

along this and head N to reach, in about 2¹/₂km, the bridge over the railway which you crossed over earlier to return across the White Bridge.

Pick up the Way again turning left towards Tyndrum; crossing hummocky sands (relics of glacial deposition), the route traverses Dalrigh, the "Kings Field" where Robert the Bruce was defeated in battle in 1306. The approach to Tyndrum is via a barren area, a legacy of the former lead mining industry here in the eighteenth century. Shortly the station is reached through the woods and a wicket gate by the level crossing.

14. CONONISH from TYNDRUM

SEE MAP C p50

ROUTE REVIEW

Station:	Tyndrum Lower
Distance:	6km (3¹/₂ miles); 100m ascent
Grade:	Easy
Map:	OS Landranger 50
Terrain:	good forest and farm tracks, return on West Highland Way (well marked but muddy in places)
Estates:	Forest Enterprise (Lorne District); Cononish Farm
Refreshments:	Tyndrum - West Highlander Restaurant; Little Chef

Good forest and farm tracks offer splendid views on this route which takes the walker towards the impressive peak of Ben Lui from Tyndrum Lower Station. Return is along a section of the West Highland Way, passing through a spoil area, a relic of earlier mining activity around Tyndrum. A geological fault passes near here; Moravian rock is juxtaposed with Dalradian schist and the mining of mineralised rock took place in the past to extract lead. Plans are presently afoot for a new venture to mine gold in the Cononish valley - see Walk 10.

*   *   *

To reach the start of the walk you need to cross the railway line to the SW using the level crossing adjacent to the station. A good wide forest track leads gently upwards with immediate views of conical Ben More in the distance to the left. As you rise up the view back across Strath Fillan reveals Tyndrum Upper Station on the Fort William Line with its Swiss Chalet design station buildings and, beyond the hamlet of Clifton, the summit of Beinn Odhar (Walk 27) and the bare shoulder of Beinn Dorain (Walk 28) come into view.

The track passes between larches (deciduous conifers which burst into scented lime-green needles each spring) and spruces, and curves right; as it levels off Beinn Dubhchraig (Walk 10) can be seen ahead with newly planted lower slopes. The track takes a further bend to the right and the substantial bulk of Ben Lui (Walk 15) comes into view beyond Beinn Dubhchraig.

The gentle descent towards the River Cononish begins and, above the farm nestling beside the river, evidence can be seen on the lower slopes of Beinn Chuirn of the recent prospecting for gold alongside a deep cleft drained by the Eas Anie. Follow the track as it curves leftwards to cross a stile over a high deer fence alongside a gate; turn left on the farm road and go through a gate taking care to shut it behind you. *The terrain here contrasts with the earlier part of the walk; the river has cut through leaving terraces of a higher level behind and nearby it tumbles over a little rock sill. Across the river the edge of Coille Coire Chuilc comprising remnants of ancient Caledonian Pine forest can be seen (Walk 13).*

As the track follows down parallel to the river and then bends left across Strath Fillan you can see Ben Challum with the railway line crossing its lower slopes. The track descends easily through recent planting to pass beneath the railway and through a gate. *Around here the ground is very undulating with rounded hillocks (drumlins) of moraine and glacial silt deposited during the last ice age. In the distance beyond Strath Fillan the summit of Ben More comes into view again, followed by Stob Binnein. Nearer at hand the railway crosses a small viaduct over the River Cononish.*

About 300 metres after passing under the railway and after a left-hand curve in the track the West Highland Way is reached, marked by two posts which have thistle markers on the far side from your approach. Ahead the Way goes to Crianlarich but you turn left along its northbound route on a small stony path to return to Tyndrum. The path rises between heather-clad slopes and past a small lochan to follow along a ridge above the river, Crom Allt, a tributary of the River Fillan. The distant mountain views still catch the eye but the path is muddy in places and you need to watch your step.

The approach to Tyndrum winds through the pinewoods above the pretty river to reach the road to the station after crossing some bare ground where crushing and smelting plants operated 200 years ago.

15. TYNDRUM to DALMALLY
a) via Cononish and Allt an Rund
b) over Ben Lui (1130m) and Beinn a'Chleibh (916m)

SEE MAP C p50

ROUTE REVIEW

Stations:	**Tyndrum Lower, Dalmally**
Distance:	**a) 19km (12 miles); 270m ascent**
	b) 21km (13 miles); 1110m ascent
Grades:	**a) Moderate/Difficult**
	b) Serious
Map:	**OS Landranger 50**
Terrain:	**a) involves about 2½km of wild trackless country; this section and 2km through forest can be wet underfoot**
	b) involves steep and rocky mountain ridges
Estates:	**Ben Lui National Nature Reserve; Cononish Farm; Forest Enterprise (Lorne District)**
Refreshments:	**Dalmally - Glen Orchy Lodge Hotel (Les Routiers)**

NB. Walk 15b) can be shortened by omitting Beinn a'Chleibh, reducing the distance by 1km and the ascent by 120m

These walks follow a common route for the first 5½km past Cononish Farm, and take the A85 for their last 3km to Dalmally. This final walk alongside the A85 can be avoided by starting at Dalmally and following the routes in the opposite direction using the Post Bus from Dalmally to Succoth Lodge Road End, but whereas this direction is also more likely to have the benefit of a following wind, the views are much superior starting from Tyndrum and the full splendour of Ben Lui can be enjoyed when it is approached from the north-east.

Ben Lui (calf hill) was a major centre for Scottish climbing in the early 1890s when Tyndrum was accessible by train but the West Highland Railway had not yet reached Fort William. It is often considered to be the finest mountain in the Southern Highlands of Scotland, and this will be appreciated when it is seen from Strath Fillan. Whilst there are good views of it from both the A85 and the train to Oban, it is seen better from the Fort William train as it traverses the hillside on the opposite side of Strath Fillan. Of considerable bulk, it holds snow, particularly in its north-east corrie, often into May, and is a mountain to be taken very seriously by the hill-walker, particularly when snow remains on it. Alternative a) offers a route beneath Ben Lui for the less ambitious hillwalker or an option should bad weather render the tops inadvisable. We also describe a route down to Glen Lochy from Ben Lui, omitting Beinn a'Chleibh but the full walk offers both another Munro and the opportunity to remain on the high tops for longer and reduce the length of the road walk to Dalmally.

Its snow-holding properties are perhaps a contributory factor in producing the abundant alpine flora on Ben Lui leading to its designation as a National Nature Reserve. Its northern cliff edges are graced by varieties of saxifrage and the lesser known wintergreen, saw-wort and rosewood amongst other species - to be admired in situ only (see Country Code).

* * *

From Tyndrum Lower Station cross to the SW side of the line using the level crossing and follow the forest road leading S up through the coniferous plantation (the start of Walk 14). When it first levels off, after about 1km, there are excellent views of Beinn Dubhchraig directly ahead; as it climbs again and turns further to the right the majestic Ben Lui comes into view. The forest road now leads down to the River Cononish.

Cononish Farm is seen ahead with evidence of mining activity above it on the slopes of Beinn Chuirn. There has been mining activity around here for some centuries and a number of disused mines are shown on the

Bridge over River Lochy

1:25,000 map, but in recent years exploration has indicated that gold may be extracted commercially and there has been renewed activity (see Walks 10 & 14).

The gravel road emerges from the plantation through a gate, and meets the farm road to Cononish; turn right on this, and after passing between the farm and farm buildings, continue for a further 2km. Ben Lui ahead continues to attract the eye, but Ben Oss (Walk 10) which has previously been hidden also comes into view on the left as the track gradually ascends until a point is reached where the main track turns downhill to the left and a less distinct track goes on ahead.

Option a) via Allt an Rund

Follow the less distinct track ahead towards the burn, but shortly before reaching it bear right to follow a line of ruined fence posts parallel to it. This is wild country and leads in about 1¹/₂km to a pass on the watershed between the drainage system via the River Tay to the North Sea and that westwards via the River Lochy to Loch Etive. From here views ahead open up dramatically of Loch Awe and Beinn a'Bhuiridh, the southernmost peak of the Cruachan group.

The way down from here is clear - head W to the point where the burn, the Eas Daimh, enters the forest and then follow a path along the N side of this burn through the plantation. When the railway is reached, there is an underpass which the Eas Daimh flows through, and the River Lochy can usually be forded at this point to reach the A85; alternatively there is a footbridge over the river about 1km to the SW. (The route along the river bank to the footbridge is rough going in places with tussocky grass and requires a series of tributaries to be crossed.)

Rather than walk all the way to Dalmally along the A85 (almost 8km), the old military road offers an alternative for about 3km through the forest on the N side of the road. It leads off from the A85 about 250 metres from the confluence of the Eas Daimh and the River Lochy, but if the footbridge has been used to cross the River Lochy it is necessary to head up through a break in the trees to join it. After re-joining the A85 about 1km E of its junction with the B8074, the main road must be followed past the Forestry offices at Corryghoil, but there is a possibility of leaving the road after this to follow the river bank for about 1km before the final stretch on a footpath alongside the road to Dalmally station.

Option b) over Ben Lui and Beinn a'Chleibh

To ascend Ben Lui follow the track downhill to cross the Allt an Rund alongside a sheep fank and then follow a path steeply up into Coire Gaothaich with the burn tumbling down from it on your left. When the gradient eases in the corrie, bear to the right and climb steeply up rough ground to reach the bounding ridge (leading NNE to Stob Garbh) at a col. There is a distinct path up this steep rocky ridge which will give the walker confidence during the ascent to the cairn on the North Top (sometimes referred to as the North West Top) and then, following the rim of the corrie, to the summit. Ben Lui being the highest mountain hereabouts, there are excellent views from it in all directions.

There are now two alternatives for the descent; **either** down to the Eas Daimh to join route a) to Dalmally, **or** over Beinn a'Chleibh (hill of the chest) and down to Succoth Lodge.

For the most straightforward descent from Ben Lui, omitting

Beinn a'Chleibh, return to the North Top but then head NW, following a path down the stony NNW ridge with the corrie which faces N on your right. The lower part of this ridge is very steep with a series of cliffs, so it is important to leave it about $^1/_2$km from the North Top (and 200m below it), and turn to the left (W) to descend via grassy slopes to the forest. A faint path may be found down these grassy slopes leading to the forest fence.

There is a stile over this fence on the E side of the burn draining Fionn Choirei (at GR 249266), and a path leads down through the forest on the right-hand side of the burn; a wide break has been established on either side of the burn, giving an open aspect, with just a few rowan trees providing a splash of colour in autumn, but the path is muddy in places. About 1km after crossing the fence the confluence with the Eas Daimh is reached; cross to the N side of the Eas Daimh and follow route (a), reaching the railway line in just over $^1/_2$km and continuing to Dalmally.

To continue over Beinn a'Chleibh head WSW from the summit of Ben Lui down a wide rocky slope, taking care not to stray to the right where there are crags. The grassy col between the two mountains is about 1km from the summit of Ben Lui and some 450m below it, and from here an easy ridge continues ahead to the rather flat summit of Beinn a'Chleibh where it is difficult to decide which cairn marks the highest point.

For the descent, proceed WNW for about 250 metres along fairly level ground and then turn to the left (W) along the S side of a very broad grassy ridge - the ground should be falling away to your left. Below is the valley of the Allt a'Chaorainn (Walk 16) which is forested in its lower part. The trees at the eastern end of the forest enclosure are stunted with plenty of space between, so there is little problem in descending through them, but the best point to head for is the low point on the forest fence at GR 231254; the valley of the burn which crosses the fence just to the N of this provides a suitable way down to the wide ride along the line of the electricity pylons, which can be followed for $^3/_4$km to a forest road. Turning to the right along this leads past Succoth Lodge and under the railway to the A85 opposite Corryghoil, just a little over 3km from Dalmally Station.

71

16. DALMALLY to ARDLUI via SUCCOTH LODGE and INVERARNAN

| SEE MAP C p50 |

ROUTE REVIEW

Stations:	Dalmally, Ardlui
Distance:	24km (15 miles); 520m ascent
Grade:	Difficult
Map:	OS Landranger 50
Terrain:	includes remote wild country without paths where accurate navigation is important
Estates:	Forest Enterprise (Lorne District); Glenfalloch*; Ben Lui National Nature Reserve (* - see Appendix B)
Refreshments:	Inverarnan - Drovers Inn; Stagger Inn Ardlui - Bothan Loch Laomainn; Ardlui Hotel

"A fine cross-country route .... following the line of an old drove road from Dalmally to Glen Falloch" (SMC Guide) over the watershed between two drainage systems - one to Loch Awe and one to Loch Lomond.

The route starts with some 3km along the main (A85) road towards Tyndrum. Part of this can be avoided after the footpath alongside the road ends by following alongside the River Orchy, but a better alternative is perhaps to avail oneself of the Post Bus which is timetabled to leave Dalmally shortly after the arrival of the morning train from Glasgow, and which will take you to Succoth Lodge Road End. The old drove road route passes through remote country to reach the A82 at Inverarnan, some 3km N of Ardlui Station.

* * *

The route leaves the A85 at GR 193275 and follows the forest road to Succoth Lodge, turning left over a bridge after 1³/₄km (just after a stone enclosure on the right) and passing under the railway where it crosses the Eas a'Ghaill. At Succoth Lodge continue ahead between farm buildings and cottages through the forest plantation to the point where the track meets the overhead pylon line; there is a small enclosure with meteorological instruments here. Continue up beneath the power lines, through the gap in the plantation where there are tracks made by all-terrain vehicles. There are fine views back towards Ben Cruachan (Walk 22). The planted trees become more stunted and about $1^{1}/_{2}$km after the met. station the fence enclosing the plantation is reached with a gate enabling you to pass through it.

From here the power lines lead somewhat left up the slope, but the Allt a'Chaorainn can be followed to the rather wet and peaty watershed. There are views ahead here of the Arrochar Alps (Walks 5,6 & 8). It is essential here to use a compass to ensure that you proceed to the correct valley - it is very easy in this wild and desolate area to stray to the right and descend to Glen Fyne! Heading ESE should bring you roughly to the point where the overhead pylon line crosses the Allt nan Caorainn and you can then follow S down this burn to a bothy; there is a sheepfold and large fenced enclosure on the NE side of the burn opposite the bothy.

From the bothy a track follows along the S side of the Allt nan Caorainn, into which many tributaries drain from Ben Lui and Ben Oss, passing an attractive lochan on the right to a point at about 330m altitude where water is diverted for the Loch Sloy hydroelectric scheme (see Walk 7). From here the track follows a pipeline down across the valley of what is now a small watercourse. *This must once have carried a major flow probably including that of the upper River Fyne up to the time when the previous west/east drainage pattern was disrupted by scouring action during the last Ice Age.*

The track climbs back up to 330m and then follows along this contour (to the left), along a series of water intakes which evenually lead through a tunnel to flow into the head of Loch Sloy. Our track, which gives access to these intakes from the A82, and affords good views across the birch wooded slopes over Glen Falloch, eventually heads downhill and swings sharply right to join another track which leads to an intake on the Allt Arnan.

Turn left at this junction and follow the track which zigzags down to the second left-hand bend (well below the pylon line) where you leave the track and go ahead descending across the slope below the pylons to pass beneath a railway bridge at GR 314186 along a track which leads to the A82, adjacent to the Stagger Inn and opposite the Drovers Inn. *(Your choice for refreshment here lies between the recently established Stagger's emphasis on Scottish fare and the*

Drover's historical ambience and long reputation as a watering hole.)

It is some 3km S from here to Ardlui Station and the A82 is a busy and dangerous road. At the time of writing the prospect of a footpath between Inverarnan and Ardlui was being explored by the Loch Lomond Park Authority and others, and hopefully by the time you are reading this there will be a footpath available for you to use. Otherwise be sure to walk along the road in single file and to face the oncoming traffic.

17. TWO SHORT WALKS from DALMALLY:

a) Dalmally Forest Walk
b) Monument Hill

> SEE MAP E p75

ROUTE REVIEW

Station:	**Dalmally**
Distance:	**a) 3km (2 miles); 90m ascent**
	b) 4km (2¹/₂ miles); 110m ascent
Grade:	**Easy**
Map:	**OS Landranger 50**
Terrain:	**a) mainly forest track, but also minor path**
	b) minor road
Estate:	**Dalmally**
Refreshments:	**Dalmally - Glen Orchy Lodge Hotel (Les Routiers)**

There are two privately owned forest estates south of Dalmally, managed by Tilhill Economic Forestry, and in 1994 plans were in hand in both for the development of woodland walks under the Woodland Grant Scheme. Here we describe both a forest walk which incorporates one of these woodland walks, and a walk along a minor road to Monument Hill, but you may find further attractive short walks hereabouts in the future.

Other points of interest at Dalmally include the fine eighteenth-century octagonal church which can be reached by a short walk to the north of the village along the B8077 to Stronmilchan. At the junction where this road leaves the village there is a curious stone, believed to be where Robert the Bruce sat around the time of his victory at the nearby Pass of Brander.

MAP E

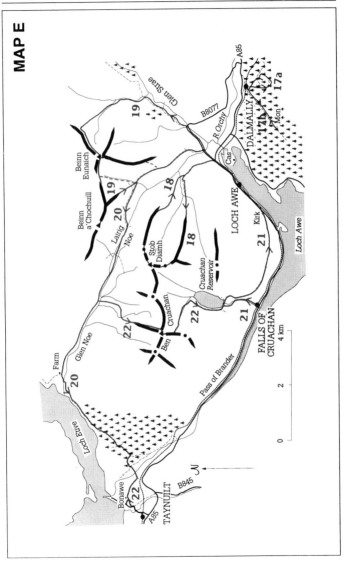

A85

Glen Strae

B8077

R. Orchy

19

Beinn
Eunaich

Beinn
a'Chochuill

Lairig
Noe

19

20

18

Stob
Diamh

18

Cas

DALMALLY

17b

Mon

17a

LOCH AWE

Kirk

21

Loch Awe

Cruachan
Reservoir

Ben
Cruachan

22

22

Glen Noe

Farm

20

22

21

FALLS OF
CRUACHAN

Pass of Brander

Loch Etive

Bonawe

22

TAYNUILT

A85

B845

0   2   4 km

a) Dalmally Forest Walk

We start with a pleasant little round through the forest on the gentle slopes above Dalmally Station.

*   *   *

From the station turn left and left again over the railway. Immediately beyond the bridge is a track leading through a parking area to a gate (Tillhill Forestry) and then upwards through the forest plantation. Continue upwards, past the track leading to the left, until the track swings round to the left and terminates. From here continue about 50 metres towards the ESE along a faint path through tussocky ground to a junction of forest rides. Turn left, towards the NE, still following a faint path, and descend the slope alongside a small stream to join another mossy forest track in about 400 metres. Turn left and in about 250 metres you will see steps leading up to the left enabling you to ascend for about 100 metres to a fine viewpoint. *The panorama here reveals much of the area of our adjacent walks and extends from Monument Hill (17b) to the west through a northern arc with the Cruachan massif (22) and the Dalmally Horseshoe (18), round to Ben Lui (15) in the east.*

Retrace your route down the steps and turn left for 10 metres on the forest track, crossing over it to follow a gravel path leading off right. This undulates through the forest to reach an open area with ruins of a settlement on a site which is thought to date back to the Iron Age. Pass beneath some overhead lines and round the far side of a square ruin where you turn half left down an ancient green track alongside an old wall. The route descends gradually, swinging right to emerge at the car park area which you left earlier. From here retrace your route back to the station.

b) Monument Hill

A visit to Dalmally is not really complete without including Monument Hill. This splendid viewpoint offers panoramic vistas and is an apt setting for a striking monument to Scotland's celebrated poet, Duncan Ban Macintyre, known affectionately as *Fairhaired Duncan of the Songs*. Duncan Ban was born in a humble croft near Victoria Bridge (see Walk 30) and spent much of his time as a stalker in the hills around Loch Tulla and Glen Orchy. His love of the

76

Monument to Duncan Ban Macintyre, Monument Hill

mountains inspired his Gaelic poetry which were transcribed by others as he was illiterate. There is an endearing anecdote about his giving a poetry "reading" in Edinburgh at which he held the book upside down!

* * *

Turn left out of the station and you will shortly see a minor road forking left and signed to the Monument. It is easy walking all the way up this metalled road with a short grassy hill to climb at the end to reach the Monument itself. Return is by the same route.

The inscription reads: "

Duncan Ban Macintyre the Glenurchay poet was born in the year 1724 and departed this life in the year 1812"

and there is a Gaelic plaque alongside.

18. DALMALLY HORSESHOE including STOB DIAMH (998m) from LOCH AWE

SEE MAP E p75

ROUTE REVIEW

Station:	**Loch Awe**
Distance:	**14km (8½ miles); 1000m ascent**
Grade:	**Serious**
Map:	**OS Landranger 50**
Terrain:	**fine ridges with steep sections (care needed in descent), approach by track.**
Estate:	**Castles Farm**
Refreshments:	**Loch Awe - Ivanhoe Buffet Car (summer); The Tight Line P.H.**

Loch Awe, one of Scotland's longest lochs, occupies a major geological syncline bounded by the superb Cruachan range of mountains to its north. Stob Diamh (pronounced "daff", peak of the stag) stands at the centre of an arc of fine ridges with two satellite tops, Stob Garbh (980m, the rough peak) and Sron an Isean (966m, nose of the gosling) which in total comprise the Dalmally Horseshoe. One joy of the route is that once an outlying top is reached there remains a mere 150m of climb to complete the horseshoe.

Although best seen as the train draws in to Dalmally Station, this fine horseshoe is most conveniently approached from Loch Awe Station, restored and reopened in May 1985. Here there are not only seasonal cruises and refreshments but also excellent views of Kilchurn Castle and, on the waterfront, a memorial to King Robert the Bruce who in 1308 won a decisive victory nearby over John of Lorn his adversary. This victory enabled King Robert to unite the Scots behind him against the English invaders.

* * *

Make your way from Loch Awe Station to the A85 and, turning right, a 15 minute walk alongside this road (there is a footpath but walk facing the traffic as far as possible!) will bring you to where the B8077 forks left and a track leads to the left through a gate (GR 134283). Follow this track, originally an old railway serving a defunct lead mine, with views of Beinn Eunaich and Beinn a'Chochuill ahead (Walk 19); as it swings round to the left, and after you have passed through a second gate, the horseshoe which has until now been hidden comes into view. Look carefully also at the slope directly ahead: after completing the horseshoe you will need to thread your way down here.

Soon you will come to a fork in the track; keep to the left, up a stony track which leads to an old quarry. *This quarry was reworked and the railway running from it reinstated when the road bridge near Kilchurn Castle was constructed during the rerouting of the main road earlier this century.* At the entrance to the quarry turn to the right, along an almost level track with old wooden sleepers across it - beware, they can be very slippery when wet. This leads in about ¹/₂km to a bridge over a burn descending from the corrie between our horseshoe and Beinn a'Bhuiridh to its left. (The track zigzags on up to the disused lead mine.)

After crossing the bridge the climb now begins up the ridge ahead; at first it is steep and our objective is hidden, but when the angle eases it comes into view again. If you pause to look back, Ben Lui (Walk 15) dominates the view behind. The broad, grassy ridge continues in a series of giant steps, with increasing numbers of boulders as the top is approached. Here a ridge coming up from the S is joined which leads fairly easily on to the summit of Stob Garbh (980m). *Mighty Ben Cruachan (Walk 22) is now seen ahead and down to the left the Cruachan Reservoir which provides the upper storage for the Cruachan power scheme, and Loch Awe winding away into the distance beyond. Behind you are the Southern Highlands.*

There is a well marked path along the ridge ahead, used by those traversing the complete Cruachan ridge. It descends N from Stob Garbh and then climbs fairly easily to the summit of Stob Diamh, the highest point of our horseshoe and a Munro. *From here Loch Etive is seen with Loch Linnhe beyond to the north-west, and to the north and north-east Ben Starav with the mountains of Glen Coe and the Black Mount beyond.* There is a steep descent from this summit towards the ENE before the final climb onto Sron an Isean. *Below on the left here you will see Coire Lochain and Glen Noe leading down to Loch Etive (Walk 20), and this final summit provides an excellent viewpoint for Beinn a'Chochuill and Beinn Eunaich (Walk 19).*

The descent from Sron an Isean is down a delightful, well-defined, and mainly grassy and easy-angled ridge. Like most such ridges hereabouts, however, the lower part has been steepened by glacial erosion during the Ice Age, forming a "truncated spur" and care is needed. The profile here is convex, a potentially dangerous situation in descent as the steeper ground below cannot be seen; it is probably best to keep to the left down through a line of crags. As you get onto easier ground below, aim to the left of all of the mine and quarry workings opposite (noting the gaping hole of the mine entrance on the right), to reach the Allt Coire Chreachainn about 200 metres above its confluence with the Allt Mhoille where (at the time of writing) there was a choice of two footbridges - the lower one appears the more secure. From here it is just 100 metres or so to the track leading to the old quarry and lead mine, and retracing your steps along this leads back to the A85 and Loch Awe Station.

19. BEINN EUNAICH (988m) & BEINN a'CHOCHUILL (980m) from LOCH AWE

SEE MAP E p75

ROUTE REVIEW

Station:	Loch Awe
Distance:	19km (12 miles); 1164m ascent
Grade:	Serious
Map:	OS Landranger 50
Terrain:	the route involves tracks and small paths, and some route finding on steepish ground with no path. Bikes could be useful for 2km each way on roads
Estates:	Glenstrae (Duiletter); Castles Farm
Refreshments:	Loch Awe - Ivanhoe Buffet Car (summer); The Tight Line P.H.

NB. It is possible to shorten this walk by omitting Beinn a'Chochuill; reducing the distance by 4km and the ascent by 260m

From Loch Awe Station a good round route may be followed over Beinn Eunaich (fowling hill) and Beinn a'Chochuill (hill of the hood) and this forms an attractive alternative to the better known Dalmally Horseshoe (see Walk 18) or the demanding excursion on the Cruachan Range (see Walk 22). The views are excellent and you may have them all to yourself! The two mountains are largely formed by granite but Beinn Eunaich has a distinctive porphyry outcrop on its NE shoulder where the "Black Shoot" has taunted many would-be climbers.

It is perhaps appropriate as you climb Beinn Eunaich to pay homage to Percy Unna who took his last walk here, failing to return. Unna devoted much of his considerable wealth to the purchase of large mountain areas of Scotland (including Glencoe) for hillwalkers by means of donations to the National Trust for Scotland. Unna had clear ideas of land management and stipulated that the hills remain in "primitive" condition with no introduction of stiles, bridges, cairns, etc. nor path improvement. The NTS has seen fit to bend the so-called "Unna Rules" somewhat, not least in the continual battle with footpath erosion.

* * *

Make your way from Loch Awe Station to the A85 and, turning right, a 15-minute walk alongside this road (there is a footpath but walk facing the traffic as far as possible!) will bring you to where the B8077 forks left to Stronmilchan. Turn left down here and after about 1/2km note the track from Castles Farm along which you will return. Continue along the road, past the electricity substation (amongst some trees) to a sharp bend in the road where a track, signed "Private Road", goes off left, leading up Glen Strae. Turn along this gravel track, passing a lochan on your right, a plantation on your left, followed by another lochan to your right - in all about 2km - until you reach a bridge, about 1/2km from the end of the plantation.

The track continues on over the bridge but you turn left on a small path alongside the burn, Allt Dhoirrean (a route over Lairig Dhoirrean to Glen Kinglass). It is wet in parts and there are a few cairns; continue for about 1 1/2km, crossing some small burns until you reach a large one draining out of Coire na Garbhliach (GR 154321). Leave the present path and follow up the burn, crossing to the other side at a convenient point and ascending the grassy ridge

Across Loch Etive from Beinn Eunaich

on the right (which is quite steep) to scramble up some bands of rock and reach an unnamed top at about 875m.

Turn left on the path along the ridge to a bealach at 805m and then proceed up the fine NE ridge of Beinn Eunaich to the summit at 988m. *Superb views abound - north across Glen Kinglass to the remote mountains beyond, west across the Lairig Noe (Walk 20) to the long finger of Loch Etive, with Stob Diamh and the pointed peaks of the massive Cruachan range (Walks 18 & 22) to its left, and eastwards the more distant summits of Ben Lui (Walk 15), Beinn Dubhchraig and Ben More, with the head of Loch Awe near at hand to the south.*

A descent can be made from Beinn Eunaich if Beinn a'Chochuill is to be omitted and there are two alternatives for this:

Alternative a): A broad grassy ridge leads S at a gentle angle with a faint path among the feldspar rocks. There is no obvious crest but follow the ridge down curving first right and then left to some peat hags on a flatter section. Cross these keeping right of a knoll just beyond. There are a series of gullies and rocky outcrops towards the end of the ridge and the ground steepens significantly. Thread your way carefully down to the right before the final outcrop which falls away quite steeply. You should be able to see the track below leading down from the Lairig Noe; pick the easiest route down to this.

Alternative b): The second route of descent is from the bealach between Beinn Eunaich and Beinn a'Chochuill. For this take the path from Beinn Eunaich summit westwards, stony and steeply down to the bealach at about 725m and then turn S and continue steeply down following the Allt Lairig Ianachain.

To ascend Beinn a'Chochuill first descend steeply W down the stony path to the bealach at 725m; an ascent for some 2km up the ridge ahead leads via a steepish top at about 900m (GR 117326) to Beinn a'Chochuill at 980m. *From here the views extend down Loch Etive to Connel Bridge and out to Mull and the Sound of Mull, with Arran in the distant south-west.*

To descend return to the 900m top and then head SE down a well-defined grassy ridge. It is fairly steep but the "hummocky" nature provides the opportunity to pick your route and there is a faint path at times. Cross the upper Hydro Board road to join the main lower one by a bridge over Allt Lairig Ianachain. Turn left and follow the track, slightly uphill at first, down through a series of gates and past Castles Farm to the B8077. *Picturesque Kilchurn Castle, a mid-fifteenth-century tower house, stands out prominently - and perhaps atmospherically in certain lighting conditions - on Loch Awe below. Built by Sir Colin Campbell in 1450 it occupies a strategic position on the upper loch and, although derelict, is well maintained. (If time and energy permit the castle can be visited free by making a detour left along the A85 for about ³⁄₄km and taking the footpath just after the bridge.)* Then retrace your route to the station.

20. LOCH AWE to TAYNUILT over the LAIRIG NOE

SEE MAP E p75

ROUTE REVIEW

Stations:	Loch Awe, Taynuilt
Distance:	20km (12½ miles); 530m ascent
Grade:	Moderate/Difficult
Map:	OS Landranger 50
Terrain:	mainly gravelled track with some rough ground over Lairig

Noe
Estates: **Castles Farm; Glenoe**
Refreshments: Taynuilt - Station Tap (West Highland Brewery)

The route over the Lairig Noe affords not only a fine low level route for the less ambitious walker wishing to sample this superb area, but also excellent views and the intrigue of walking from a freshwater loch (Loch Awe) to the magnificently situated sea loch, Loch Etive. Loch Etive represents a long finger of sea reaching inland for some 36km from Connel (see Walk 23) and this walk follows along its south bank for some distance before reaching Taynuilt (an inn by the stream) across the River Awe. There is opportunity if time permits to visit Bonawe iron furnace which operated from 1753 to 1876 near the pier en route to Taynuilt. The iron smelting process used charcoal and required five tons of timber to smelt each ton of pig iron so, not surprisingly it led to extensive deforestation of the area. A main product of the furnace was cannon balls, allegedly including those fired at the Battle of Trafalgar. Recently restored and now in the care of Historic Scotland, the Bonawe complex is open from April to September.

* * *

From Loch Awe Station make your way to the A85 and turn right, following the A85 and B8077 for some 2km (see the first paragraph of Walk 19) as far as the entrance to Castles Farm. Turn left along the farm track crossing the cattle grid and past some fine pines, to follow the track to a junction shortly before the farm. Bear left here onto a gravel and stone track. After passing through two gates the track rises steadily winding round beneath Beinn Eunaich and Beinn a 'Chochuill (Walk 19). Fine views to the rear across Loch Awe may be seen including Kilchurn Castle and Monument Hill (Walk 17b) beyond.

The track crosses a burn, descending from Beinn a'Chochuill, and levels off, descending slightly to reach a hut. *This belongs to Scottish Power who took over the operation of Cruachan hydro-electric scheme from the North of Scotland Hydro Electric Board in 1990. The Cruachan scheme works by pump storage with a reservoir hidden away some 400m up in Ben Cruachan with a feed shaft to the power station below on Loch Aweside. The network of tracks used on this walk forms part of the servicing infrastructure for additional water intake for the reservoir (see also Walk 21).* Continue on past the water take-off points and just before the track crosses a bridge a series of stout posts leads up right to the Lairig Noe. Follow the posts to cross the watershed at around 570m; there is no clear track and it is rough and often wet ground but the going is not difficult.

Continue to follow the posts descending towards the headwater burns of the River Noe, taking care to avoid a deep and dangerous gully well to the left of the posted route. After about ¹/₂km from the col there is a short stretch of track contouring round the hillside; turn right on this and just before it crosses a burn turn off left over rough ground to follow the left bank of the burn. Follow down alongside the burn for some 1¹/₂km until it meets the main river coming in from the left. At this point the burn you have been following is boulder-strewn and you should cross it and head slightly rightwards to meet some twin (wheel) tracks heading down the valley about 100 metres to the right of and parallel to the river. These, made by an all-terrain Scottish Power service vehicle, offer a clear, if not always dry, route down Glen Noe and there is ample scope on this easier ground to enjoy the fine view which may be had of the massive cliffs and corries of the Cruachan range towering above to the left of the glen (see Walk 22).

In due course a narrow footpath along the river bank offers firmer walking. Take this path and follow the river down as it tumbles over the rocky ground until you meet a farm track leading around some sheep pens. Bear right here, following the track across a burn and pass through two gates to reach Glennoe Farm, located on the long track which follows the S bank of Loch Etive.

Turn left crossing a bridge over the River Noe and along the track which undulates above Loch Etive, giving pretty views across this remote Loch whose sheltered waters are used here for fish farming. Pass through a gate into Inverawe forest; this is a working forest and you should take extra care if timber operations are in progress. Continue on for about 2km, passing tracks on your right and left to reach a tarmac, walled road running between Inverawe House and Bridge of Awe.

Turn right on this road and follow it downhill to a T-junction;

turn left here for about 25 metres and then right at a white cottage along a track leading to a footbridge over the River Awe. Continue up the far side to the left of a fence to reach a lane; turn right along this passing the grounds of Bonawe House, a mansion built for the iron foundry manager and once described by Dorothy Wordsworth as "an ugly yellow-daubed building, staring this way and that". Then keep left along a track past some cottages; these units, comprising a single living room with sleeping loft above, were built as simple accommodation for the furnace workers. The main Bonawe Furnace Museum complex is located a short way along on the right. Continue ahead on the minor road from Bonawe to reach a junction with the B845 leading from Taynuilt to the pier on Loch Etive. Turn left along this road and then right at a T-junction to reach the station in some 400 metres. The station buildings are now the home of the West Highland Brewers whose product is available along with bar snacks etc. at the Station Tap, and you can visit the brewery.

21. FALLS of CRUACHAN to LOCH AWE via CRUACHAN RESERVOIR

SEE MAP E p75

ROUTE REVIEW

Stations:	Falls of Cruachan (summer service only), Loch Awe
Distance:	8km (5 miles); 360m ascent
Grade:	Moderate
Map:	OS Landranger 50
Terrain:	ascent by small path, steep at times and muddy in places; descent via tarmac road
Estate:	Castles Farm
Refreshments:	Loch Awe - Ivanhoe Buffet Car (summer); The Tight Line P.H.

The Falls of Cruachan Station is operational only during daylight hours in the summer months and then for request stops only (see Scotrail Timetable). Its use enables an attractive walk to be done ascending alongside the Falls towards the reservoir Dam and affording excellent views from the Scottish Power service road while descending to Loch Awe Station. It is possible to combine this walk with a visit to the Cruachan Pump Storage Power Station, or to St Conan's Kirk; you can also travel back in time with a cruise aboard the little steamboat from Loch Awe pier and refreshments in the Pullman carriage (Ivanhoe) - both operating alongside the station in summer.

Cruachan Reservoir was constructed in the 1960s as part of the hydroelectric pump storage scheme largely secreted within the mountain itself such that Ben Cruachan has been dubbed "The Hollow Mountain". Opened in 1965 the scheme generates around 450 million units of electricity per annum, supplying electricity to Scotland at peak demand periods while pumping water from Loch Awe back up to the reservoir at other times. The reversible turbine generators are housed in a huge machine hall located 1km inside the mountain and some 400m below the surface. The reservoir capacity is 10 million cubic metres of water, equivalent to 83.3 million units of electricity. Scottish Power offer guided tours into the power station complex within the mountain, from the Visitors' Centre across the road from the station.

St Conan's Kirk, located near to where the private Scottish Power road joins the main A85, is deceptive in appearance being dedicated for worship as recently as 1930, despite its air of antiquity. Its establishment arose when the coming of the railway alongside Loch Awe made the area far more accessible for habitation, with potentially viable support for the church. It is believed that Walter Campbell built the original simple church here to save his mother the long journey to church in Dalmally from their island home on Innischonain. He then designed the present elaborate building which became his life's work, completed after his death by his sister and their Trustees. A very informative booklet for visitors is available inside.

* * *

From the Falls of Cruachan Station go beneath the underpass, and follow the small path (leading NW above the railway) which very shortly passes under a set of vertical wires. *Following a series of derailments prior to the turn of the century these steel "piano" wires, as they were called, were installed for some 5km alongside this section of the railway running through the Pass of Brander where the slopes rise steeply above. Any rockfall disturbing the wires triggered a signal alerting the train driver that there may be debris on the line.*

The route goes up some steps past a generator and through the native birch and oak woods on a gently rising path. After crossing a ditch with a pipe in it, fork right by a post (where a path goes ahead towards a thick trunked oak tree). Our path now ascends more steeply up a tree clad ridge with the Falls to the left. The view below still includes the western arm of Loch Awe which drains seawards via the River Awe and Loch Etive but as you leave the trees and zigzag up through the bracken you can see the extensive southern reaches of Loch Awe come into view behind you. Below the Power Station Visitor Centre is the point where water is taken from and returned to Loch Awe and above you is the road to the dam, the route of descent. Soon the gradient eases and the path contours round the hillside; care should be taken as the path is breaking away in places. In clear weather the shoulder of Ben Cruachan can be seen ahead.

The route goes over boggy ground to emerge alongside a rocky section of the burn, interspersed with pools. Some metal girders span the burn, relics of a now defunct bridge. The path over the flattest section of the route becomes less distinct but if you keep alongside the burn you should avoid the wettest ground and shortly reach the private tarmac road at the bridge over the burn. You can turn right to descend directly to Loch Awe Station from here, but our route continues up to the reservoir and crosses the top of the dam wall. For this turn left on the road and in due course make your way up over steepish rough ground to gain the left edge of the walled spillway from the reservoir; you reach the road leading from the Dam by crossing the spillway. (If this is carrying water, then you can reach the dam wall by a ladder to the right.) The walk across the dam affords superb views of the horseshoe of mountains which surround the reservoir. At the end turn down the tarmac road to a junction where you continue ahead.

Follow the tarmac road as it winds down the steep hillside; from this lofty position it is hard to remember that the western arm of Loch Awe is tucked away beneath the slopes until it comes into view as the road traverses round. A substantial barrier flanks the road and where this ends there is a small cairn just above to the right; the few steps up to here are well worth taking to enjoy the fine panoramic view of the Loch with its islands clustered at the bend.

Legend has it that Loch Awe was formed by a witch who used to graze her favourite cow up on Ben Cruachan; the cow drank from a magic well which overflowed while the witch slept and the waters rushed down to flood the valley; hence Loch Awe came into being.

The road descends and as it curves leftwards Ben Lui (Walk 15) comes into view in the distance. Nearer at hand can be seen Monument Hill (see Walk 17b), and as you descend further, there is a fine view of Kilchurn Castle at the head of Loch Awe (see Walk 19). Go through the gate at the end of the road, alongside the multi-padlocked vehicle gate (one lock for each authorised user!), and continue downhill to reach the main road near to St Conan's Kirk. Continue along the pavement to the left for about 1km to reach Loch Awe Station.

22. TAYNUILT to FALLS of CRUACHAN (or LOCH AWE) over BEN CRUACHAN (1126m)

SEE MAP E P75

ROUTE REVIEW

Stations:	Taynuilt, Falls of Cruachan (summer service only) or Loch Awe
Distance:	18km (11 miles) to Falls of Cruachan or 23km (14½ miles) to Loch Awe; 1200m ascent
Grade:	Serious
Map:	OS Landranger 50
Terrain:	involves a steep ascent up a rocky and sometimes narrow ridge; a mountain bike can be used as far as Glennoe Farm (7km) and back, in which case the route to the summit (more difficult down than up) would need to be reversed, returning to Taynuilt Station
Estates:	Glenoe; Glenstrae (Cruachan); Castles Farm
Refreshments:	Loch Awe - Ivanhoe Buffet Car (summer); The Tight Line P.H.

Ben Cruachan (1126m, stacky hill) has been called "The Hollow Mountain" since the construction of the Cruachan pumped storage hydroelectric scheme (see Walks 20 & 21). Together with its neighbouring peaks it forms one of the most impressive mountain ranges in Scotland and the approach from Taynuilt, alongside Loch Etive offers a spectacular, strenuous and long expedition. The descent is via the reservoir to Falls of Cruachan Station (which is open only in summer) or to Loch Awe Station. The extensive Cruachan massif, composed of jagged granite ridges on a dioritic rock base, is bounded by deep glens (Pass of Brander and Glen Strae) and Lochs Etive and Awe. The route described here is an airy mountaineering classic requiring plenty of stamina and you should allow ample time, especially in winter.

*   *   *

From Taynuilt Station turn left along the B845 towards the jetty on Loch Etive. Cross the river and turn left at a junction (signed to Bonawe Furnace) up a hill and very shortly turn right past a church continuing on to pass Bonawe Furnace on the left. (For further information about Bonawe see Walk 20.) Keep right in front of some cottages, leaving Bonawe House to your left, and continue along a lane to a gate in the fence on your left, at a bend (shortly before the lane crosses the railway). Turn through the gate and go down the field with a fence on your left to cross a footbridge over the River Awe. When you reach the road at Inverawe where there is a white cottage, turn left for about 25 metres and then sharp right on a road going up hill. Follow round a right-hand bend and in 400 metres turn left up a forest road, gated a short way along. Keep left where a new forest road goes right and then keep right at the next junction through the plantation. If timber felling operations are in progress take care to comply with any directions.

Shortly after a second gate the track emerges into open mixed woodland and descends to follow the shore of Loch Etive through a third gate. Passing a modern bungalow on the right, continue to follow the road swinging away from the Loch and crossing a bridge over the River Noe. This brings you to Glennoe Farm.

Turn right at the farm to leave the farm house and buildings on your left and continue up the track through gates until this ends at some sheep pens in about 700 metres. Here a green track continues ahead and there are superb views up the Lairig Noe, flanked by Beinn a'Chochuill (see Walk 19) to the left and the massive bulk of the Cruachan range on the right. Pleasant walking with the River Noe on your right past a tumbling waterfall brings you to its junction with a tributary, Allt Garbh in a small gorge. Above this and after the next major right-hand burn junction, take the first opportunity to cross the river (this is some 3 km from Glennoe Farm), and begin to climb up heading S.

Two burns drain down Coire Caorach; keep between them but closer to the E one. After rounding a knoll cross over the burn on your W on flat ground and begin the ascent of the North Ridge which is grassy and boulder strewn. At about 900m the ridge narrows and drops away steeply particularly on the E side - care is needed along here. A fairly level stretch leads to a steeper rise to gain the main summit ridge. Turn right along this, and after a short scramble of 200-300 metres the summit (of markedly pink granite) is reached. *In clear weather this vantage point affords a rewarding panorama with mountain ranges surrounding three sides and an unrivalled view seawards of the islands of the Inner Hebrides.*

From the summit, heading S down a cairned path along a wide ridge with rocks and boulders brings you to a bealach with a fence and a stile; turn down to your left following the cairned route, steeply at first and keeping left, cross over a burn and zigzag down. About 1km below the bealach the path crosses to the S side of the burn; continue down, swinging right to join the vehicle track which is followed round the reservoir to the dam.

Here the routes to Falls of Cruachan Station and Loch Awe Station diverge:

a) Descent to Falls of Cruachan Station (trains only stop here when requested during daylight in summer)

From the W end of the dam head down, across the spillway, to join the road some 50m below. (If water is flowing down the spillway it can be crossed on the dam and the descent made to the roadway by ladder and steps.) Follow the road for about 400 metres to a bridge over a burn (just after passing the point where the electricity transmission lines from the power station are brought to the surface and are lead away to the SE by the "striding" pylons). Paths lead down to the A85 road on either side of this burn, though only that on the W side is shown on the OS map. To reach the station it is preferable to take that on the E side of the burn. This becomes distinct a short way below the bridge, and then after a gradual descent traverses to the left above a steep slope before a zig-zag descent first down a bracken-covered slope (when the arm of Loch Awe extending into the Pass of Brander comes into view), and then through oak and birch woodland alongside the rocky gorge containing the Falls of Cruachan. As the railway line is approached the path swings to the left and passes under the "piano wires" before reaching an underpass beneath the railway which leads directly to the steps up to the station platform. (See Walk 21 for a description of this route in reverse.)

The Falls of Cruachan Visitor Centre is located immediately across the road from the station. Scottish Power offer guided tours of the pump storage scheme within the mountain (see Walk 21).

b) Descent to Loch Awe Station

Cross the dam, a good point for a view back to the summit, and then take the Scottish Power metalled road leading southwards and eastwards down to the main A85 road. This easy going descent follows the route described in the last paragraphs of Walk 21 and the introduction to that walk also features St Conan's Kirk to which a visit may be made if time permits.

23. OBAN to TAYNUILT via GLEN LONAN

SEE MAP F p94

ROUTE REVIEW

Stations:	Oban, Taynuilt
Distance:	18km (11 miles); 230m ascent
Grade:	Easy
Map:	OS Landranger 49
Terrain:	mainly minor roads - bikes are ideal for this route
Refreshments:	Oban Rare Breeds Park - tearoom
	Taynuilt - Station Tap (West Highland Brewery)

Oban is often known as the "Gateway to the Isles", but for this branch of the railway it marks the end of the line at the station near the heart of this busy little town with its attractive harbour. Indeed, part of the name "Ob" - originating from the Vikings - means a sheltered bay where ships can overwinter.

This lovely route via Glen Lonan follows minor roads and out of the busy tourist season it makes a good walk. It starts by exploring one of the attractions of Oban, a major landmark above the town known as McCaig's Tower; in 1895 John Stuart McCaig, a wealthy Oban banker, began the building of the tower as a work scheme for unemployed local craftsmen. By 1900 his rather grandiose schemes for a museum and art gallery were shelved but later its promise as an observation point was realised by the local Council and the now landscaped environs offer a very fine panoramic view of the Highlands and Islands.

The Glen Lonan route is also an excellent one for cyclists for whom an alternative way out of Oban is described. Barguillean Gardens with mossy walks, a wild wood and profusion of spring flowers, located about 5km before Taynuilt, can be visited for a small charge.

*   *   *

For those on foot McCaig's Tower is the first objective on leaving the station, so head N alongside the harbour on George Street until you reach Argyll Street, a right turn half way along the harbour. At the end turn left a short way to reach a steep flight of steps, Jacob's Ladder, leading up the cliff face, Creag a'Bharrain. A small iron gate leads out onto Ardconnel Terrace; turn left and then right at the junction into Laurel Road, which passes directly beneath McCaig's Tower. There is a large car park from which a flight of steps gives access to the interior of the granite tower.

From here turn right into Duncraggan Road and at its end turn left into Ardconnel Road; after Rockfield Road joins from the right there is a path immediately opposite with steps leading upwards. Follow this between the gardens and across a road, the driveway to Ardconnel House, continuing on to join a private road which descends steeply and bends round to the right. Cross the cattle grid to the left into some pasture land where horses and sheep may be

MAP F

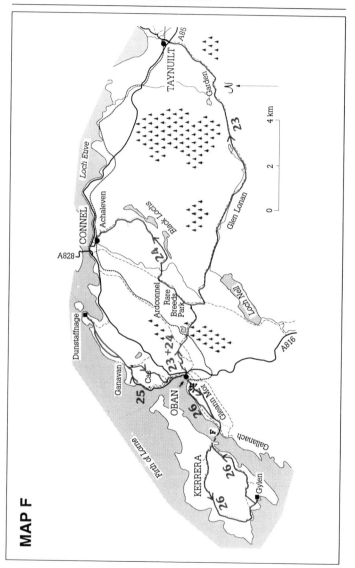

grazing and follow a track leading to Polvinister cottage, once the site of a market stance on the drovers' route which passed this way. Go through the two gates and follow along a green track, turning right at a ruined barn to reach a gate behind some houses. Passing through this continue down the lane to a road junction, where you keep ahead.

For the cyclist the route from Oban Station passes through Argyll Square, heading S along Combie Street and forks left in front of Kilmore and Oban Parish Church. Follow along Glen Cruitten Road which passes beneath the steep crags of Craig a'Chait (the rock of the wild cat). Ignoring the steep turn to the left (which leads to the hospital), continue along the Glen with the Golf Course presided over by the Iron Age fortress of Dunans on your right until you reach a junction where you take the right turn towards Taynuilt.

The minor road to the SE crosses the golf course and passes beneath the railway to zigzag up past a lochan on the left and the fine Glencruitten House on the right. There is a small area of forestry before the route continues through open land with wide views. *This type of forest edge is home to buzzards and you may be lucky enough to see this large bird of prey soaring above.*

Some 300 metres beyond the Oban Rare Breeds Park turn right at a T-junction towards Kilmore (the left turn goes via Ardconnel to Connel - see Walk 24), and after just over $1/2$km turn left for Taynuilt (signed - $7^1/2$ miles) on to an unfenced road. The road winds past some ancient cairns and a standing stone via the head of Loch Nell towards the wooded slopes of Glen Lonan ahead. The valley, narrow at first then opening out, is drained by a delightful river with some lush pasture around Glenamachrie. The road is flanked by young coniferous plantation to the left and deciduous woodland to the right. Crossing a bridge the road continues over marshy ground - perhaps a previous loch bed - and Deadh Choimhead dominates above on the left while there are some fine mature conifer specimen trees on the right. A small lochan precedes more pastureland before the wooded hill of Am Barr is reached. NE of the hill is lovely Barguillean Gardens overlooking a lochan and the nurseries.

Continue on and down the wooded slopes past Lonan House,

with holiday flats, and Airdeny chalets; there are timber works on the left and views of the towering Ben Cruachan (see Walk 22) ahead. On reaching the main A85 road, cross over to reach the station at Taynuilt. *The station buildings are now the home of the West Highland Brewers whose brew is on offer with other refreshments in the Station Tap (and you can visit the brewery).*

24. OBAN to CONNEL via ARDCONNEL and ACHALEVEN

SEE MAP F p94

ROUTE REVIEW

Stations:	Oban, Connel
Distance:	11km (7 miles); 200m ascent
Grade:	Easy
Map:	OS Landranger 49
Terrain:	minor roads, lanes and footpaths
Refreshments:	Oban Rare Breeds Park - tearoom
	Connel - Falls of Lora Hotel

Several minor roads and tracks run north-east from Oban towards Connel but the footpaths described here past the Black Lochs to Achaleven offer one of the most attractive routes. As with Walk 23, the start from Oban is via McCaig's Tower, a lofty vantage point from which to view the Isle of Mull to which ferries ply from the harbour beneath. Following its early settlement by cave-dwellers (see Walk 25) Oban has attracted visitors through the ages. More illustrious visitors have included Queen Victoria, and in 1773, Boswell and Johnson to "one tolerable inn", now the home of the Tourist Information Centre in Argyle Square. Before them were rather less welcome Vikings. Not only a seaport, Oban has also been important as a droving centre for cattle heading east from the Isles.

At Connel if time permits it is worth a short detour to see the Falls of Lora. The falls, located in the rocky narrows under the road bridge at the mouth of Loch Etive, occur when there is a marked difference in the level of water in Loch Etive compared with the tidal level outside. On a rising tide the water cascades into Loch Etive from outside and on a falling tide the water pours out of the Loch

Returning from Loch Dochard (29)
Black Rock Cottage and Buachaille Etive Mor (30)

Buachaille Etive Mor from near Kingshouse (30)
Corrour Summit with Beinn na Lap (34)

through a series of whirlpools and rapids resulting in an apparent "waterfall" in each direction. The road bridge under which they flow was built in 1900 originally to carry the (now defunct) railway line from Connel to Ballachulish.

* * *

From the station follow the route described in Walk 23 up to McCaig's Tower and onwards to the road junction by the golf course. Here the left-hand route (signed Achavaich) goes directly to Connel, closely following the railway, but our route goes ahead along the road passing through the golf course. It continues beneath the railway, to wind up a wooded slope and then through open land past the Oban Rare Breeds Park with woodland walk, nature trail and tearoom open to visitors in summer. About 300 metres beyond turn left at a T-junction towards Connel (signed 3 miles).

After passing through some patches of woodland the road becomes unfenced crossing undulating moorland. About 1½km from the junction Ardconnel is reached and shortly after this a track leads off right to Kilvaree through a gate adjacent to some caravans. Pass through, taking care to shut the gate. Follow this farm road down, across a bridge, past a ruin and round a hill. Pass by the reedy southern end of Black Lochs to reach Kilvaree Farm. Leaving the farm buildings to your right, go through a series of gates to continue along a green track heading NE along the slopes above Black Lochs from where there are pleasant views E across Fearnoch Forest. Almost 1km after Kilvaree the track swings left away from Black Lochs and then through a gate (where a faint track comes in from the left), and across a field to uninhabited Cuil-uaine cottages. There is a good farm track beyond here, crossing over heather-clad moors and then heading down to Achaleven. Turn left by the white farm buildings on to a small road and continue under the railway to the main road.

Turn left on the main road and proceed along to the Falls of Lora Hotel where you fork left to reach the village and the station.

25. GANAVAN and DUNSTAFFNAGE from OBAN

SEE MAP F p94

ROUTE REVIEW

Station:	**Oban**
Distance:	**13km (8 miles); 300m ascent**
Grade:	**Easy/Moderate**
Map:	**OS Landranger 49**
Terrain:	**Paths, tracks, road, and open moorland; bikes are suitable for the road section to and from Ganavan**
Refreshments:	**Ganavan - The Pavilion**
	Oban - plenty of choice

This coastal walk culminates in a visit to Dunstaffnage Castle, taking in the more modest Dunollie Castle en route. The latter, a thirteenth-century tower-house, built on a site where there had been a fortification since the seventh century, commands a strategic situation with views seawards to and between the islands. The Castle was abandoned in 1746 when Dunollie House (to the rear) was built as the home of the Chief of the MacDougall clan. Dunstaffnage Castle was built by the MacDougalls and remained their principal fortress until 1309 when they suffered defeat by Robert the Bruce. It occupies an even finer strategic position overlooking the mouth of Loch Etive and the meeting point of the Sound of Mull and the Firth of Lorn. It is open to visitors from April to September (small charge).

The return to Oban is over the cliff top to Ganavan from where a higher level route over the moorland tops gives ample scope to enjoy the seascape ringed with islands, and the mountains both inland and offshore. Route finding here is somewhat intricate and the easier option is merely to retrace the route of your outward walk.

* * *

From Oban Station proceed N along the harbour wall and continue along the Corran Esplanade fronting Oban Bay. Where the main road forks right towards Fort William and Glasgow, in front of Corran Halls, continue ahead along the seafront below the Halls.

You will shortly see St Columba's RC Cathedral on the right; continue on to the War Memorial alongside which is a large cup-marked boulder. Pause a while at the "plateau", a grassy area with tiny lighthouse flanked by seats and admire the seawards view with the island of Kerrera nearest at hand (see Walk 26).

The road hugs the coast, past Port Mor and on to Carraig Mhicheil, a rocky point above which towers the ruined Dunollie Castle. There is a small gate in the roadside fence, from which a path winds up the steep cliff to the castle. It is open (without charge) at all reasonable hours, but visitors go at their own risk. Continue along the road for about a further 1km, keeping left at the fork, until you reach Ganavan Bay where there may be opportunity for refreshment.

To continue on to Dunstaffnage take the clear track beneath the cliff from the N end of the Bay for about 250 metres and then strike right up a grassy incline between the rounded edges of the cliffs to follow left along the gorse fringed edge of the cliff. On reaching the top keep ahead on a wide path to the top of Ganavan Hill (72m) and be rewarded with a fine view towards Connel Bridge. The buildings on the near side of Dunstaffnage Bay are a marine laboratory. From here descend to a stile, cross this and then keep ahead over the undulating tops before descending to cross a ruined wall in a valley. Take the small path half right across the slope ahead and over the final mound and descend gently towards a walled field, passing close by a small pond on your left. Follow the wall boundary towards the cliff edge and scramble a short way down the cliff edge at the corner of the wall. Cross the metal gate (to which you will return en route back) in the fence ahead continuing over wet ground and around the bay of Camas Rubha na Liathaig. Turn right along the footpath adjacent to a small fenced plantation to reach a stile onto the minor road leading left to Dunstaffnage Castle - open to visitors with an entrance charge.

Retrace your outward route as far as the metal gate and after crossing this keep along the path beneath the cliffs following the raised beach above the present bays, coves and inlets. Continue on past pebbly beaches and between upper and lower cliffs to reach a fence descending alongside a burn. Cross the gate in the fence. Recent erosion has produced some awkward steps across a sea filled ravine on the path to Ganavan under the cliff so this route is not advised. Instead, turn left up alongside the fence and after gaining height (and when you can see the stile you crossed on the outward route) fork right on a faint path to reach the top of the cliffs. Follow along the turfed cliff tops and then descend towards Ganavan Bay, crossing the parking area and retrace your steps to the fork in the road; here turn sharply left and then swing right up the hill over the Braes of Ganavan. On leaving the houses the road passes through a gateway to rise up onto open moorland along a rough farm track leading to Dunollie Beg. (Note: it is quite possible to return to Oban proceeding along this track to the main road but you should be prepared for plenty of traffic.)

About 50 metres after the gateway you will see on the right a grassy track crossing the open land below. Make your way down to this and follow it right as it skirts a marshy area on its left. Your objective is the hill to your left with two adjacent telegraph poles near its top, so make your way up to these. It is easiest to keep somewhat to the left of the telegraph wires leading up here, and there is a faint path following the line of an old ruined wall.

The summit of Cnoc Carnach, the "Stony Hill" is marked by a metal post. *Here the surrounding views, untrammelled by urbanisation, are quite spectacular, from Oban Bay, right down the Sound of Kerrera, past the islands of Kerrera (Walk 26), Mull and Lismore, to Connel (Walk 24) and inland the unmistakable pointed peak of Ben Cruachan (Walk 22).*

From the summit the route passes through the housing estate below (left, as you face Oban Bay) and the short descent to this needs a little care as this craggy top is steeply sided. Head steeply down towards the trees to the right and then turn left on a small path which passes through a gateway to meet a private farm track. Cross over this and head diagonally down to the far corner of a small play area. Cross this into Kerrera Terrace, turning first right into Cruachan Crescent. At the end turn right on Lorn Avenue, and after passing another road on the right, fork rightish across MacDougall Court and Grahame Court to reach a small track leading past a play area and down alongside a burn. This track winds down through the woods to reach a bridge on a bridleway.

The bridleway was once a private carriageway leading to Dunollie House; now it affords a wooded walk along an old raised beach platform at the foot of the ancient sea cliffs of Craig Moraig and Barr Mor (the "Great Ridge") complete with some prehistoric caves thought to date back as long as 5000 BC, where remains of early human occupation were found (now on display in the museum at Corran Halls).

Turn left here and at Corran Brae turn right to reach the Esplanade, retracing your route back to the station. If time permits you can visit the Oban Experience Visitor Centre adjacent to the station; this is a celebration of the history of Oban with steam train reconstruction and paddle steamers.

26. ISLE of KERRERA from OBAN

SEE MAP F p94

ROUTE REVIEW

Station:	Oban
Distance:	17km (10½ miles); 320m ascent
Grade:	Easy/Moderate
Map:	OS Landranger 49
Terrain:	good tracks, green lanes and paths (wet in places)
Ferry to Kerrera:	regular service, Tel 0631 63665 (bikes may be taken)
Refreshments:	None available nearer than Oban

An island has its own special qualities and a walk around Kerrera, which can be explored only by pedestrians and cyclists yet is within a stone's throw of Oban, can be a magical experience. At 6km long and 3km wide, Kerrera is an ideal size for a day's visit and this green island, where the sheep far outnumber the 30-odd human inhabitants, is especially appealing with its rich archaeological and geological heritage and superb coastal scenery.

Access to Kerrera is via a small passenger ferry boat which operates from a jetty 3½km south of Oban on the minor coastal road from Oban to Gallanach. Cyclists can easily reach the ferry by this road but there is an attractive walk from Oban via Gleann Mor.

* * *

From the station turn towards Argyll Square (where the Tourist Information Centre is located) and immediately sharp right into

To Gallanach from Kerrera

Shore Street. Turn right at the junction and after the road crosses the railway keep ahead to a T-junction and then up Haggarts Brae, opposite, to reach Glenmore Road. Follow this right to a junction with Villa Road (which heads back sharp right). At the junction there is a stepped path leading rightish which takes you to Pulpit Hill, a landmark overlooking Oban affording excellent views interpreted by a viewpoint indicator. *Pulpit Hill is the local name of Crannaig a'Mhinisteir, literally "Priest's Rock", and legend has it that the huge stone adjacent to the viewpoint was used as a altar in pagan rituals.*

From Pulpit Hill take the road S, past the car park and toilets, forking left and then right into Pulpit Drive. Before a house on the left a track leads off left beneath a TV tower. After passing between the houses and a small lochan the route crosses Gleann Mor via an old drove road, in all probability used by pilgrims en route across Kerrera to Iona. Passing through a gate the track crosses open land and it becomes wet underfoot. Shortly after a ruined wall and at a second gate a good green track descends directly down to the slipway for the ferry to Kerrera.

After landing on the island proceed up the track to the telephone box and then keep right at the junction beyond. The track rises gently, passing to the right of the school, which in 1994 had just two pupils with a teacher coming in daily from the mainland, and through a gate on the crest to pass a track to Balliemore Farm. A short way after the farm track, views across Slatrach Bay and the sound to Mull open up ahead and as the track you are on bears right there is a gate on the left. Pass through the gate onto a green lane; this is an old drove road, a link for cattle crossing from the outer islands to the mainland. The lane contours round through open land, and then descends to Barnabuck Bay. *This was the site of an old harbour for the ferry to Mull in the eighteenth century and used for cattle landings. Only a whitewashed cottage enjoys this splendid view of the cliffs of Mull now, but once this community boasted its own brewery and still!*

Keep close by the cottage to take an upper track which rises steadily between lower and upper bluffs and curves around the hillside before heading S to Ardmore. The route makes use of the raised beaches, relics of higher sea levels, and passes through a notch with freshwater pools. At Ardmore you reach the sea again and beyond the cottage pass a remarkable rock pinnacle, a natural basalt formation which has outlasted the adjacent rock. Continue on around the coast to your left, where the shoreline features isolated rock pinnacles rising out of the sea and stark indented coves of black volcanic rock.

For even more dramatic scenery, fork right off the track at the head of a bay some 400 metres after Ardmore cottage through a gate and follow round within about 100 metres of the coast to the ruined Gylen Castle spectacularly sited as a fortress on a high knoll above the sea. *Built at the end of the sixteenth century its fate was to be beseiged and burnt half a century later and never reconstructed. It still retains architectural interest and undoubted atmosphere. The castle is an excellent vantage point from which to enjoy the views south to Seil Island, the Island of Luing and west of these, Jura, Islay and Colonsay on a clear day.*

From the castle retrace your steps a short way and then follow up the E side of a burn to rejoin the main track you left earlier just E of Lower Gylen. The track now climbs in zigzags over a small pass before passing Upper Gylen on the right. Good views across the Sound of Kerrera open up, with the castle-like Gallanach House opposite on the mainland. The track winds down to Little Horseshoe Bay, overlooked by old quarrymen's cottages, and on above the shoreline to Horseshoe Bay, just S of the jetty. *This area has historic connections, dating back to Norwegian ownership of Kerrera in the thirteenth century. In 1249 Alexander II of Scotland anchored his fleet in Horseshoe Bay, vowing to add Kerrera, along with other western isles, to his Kingdom. On landing, he was taken ill and died soon after.* It is now only a short distance back to the ferry which will transport you from the island, now a twentieth-century peaceful haven, and back to the mainland.

The return to Oban can be via the outward route or the minor road along the shore. However you can reduce the amount walked on the road by going back up the green track to the gate. Do not pass through this but keep left on a narrow path which follows along the grassy tops of the cliffs for a little over $1/2$km to a fence corner. Continue with the fence on your right for about 150 metres to a narrow steep-sided gully and follow the path down here to join the coastal road just beyond Kilbowie. It is then less than 2km back to Oban Station.

INTRODUCTION

From Crianlarich the West Highland Railway continues its gradual ascent northwards to its summit at Corrour, at 400m the highest station in the British Isles and the only one not served by any public road. The ascent is interrupted by a downhill stretch, incorporating a major viaduct, between Tyndrum and Bridge of Orchy, below high peaks which are ascended in Walks 27 and 28. Beyond Bridge of Orchy the Railway passes lovely Loch Tulla before crossing (in part via Britain's only snowshed) lonely Rannoch Moor, thanks to an imaginative railway engineering feat, to reach the remote Corrour Station. The Moor is explored in Walks 30 to 32 and Corrour Station is the starting point both for a delightful walk around Loch Ossian and for perhaps the easiest ascent of any Munro, Beinn na Lap. More challenging are the walks north from here (35 and 36), over or between the high mountains to Glen Spean. The railway descends fairly steeply above Loch Treig to Tulloch and then follows Glen Spean to Spean Bridge and on to Fort William. The fascinating Parallel Roads of Glen Roy to the north of Glen Spean are explored in Walk 37.

Whilst Ben Nevis, Scotland's highest mountain, is the goal of most hill-walkers visiting Fort William, we offer somewhat shorter and easier walks from here which can be more realistically completed after arrival on the morning train from Glasgow and in time to return on the evening train. Those wishing to ascend Ben Nevis, however, should have no difficulty in finding directions for the main "Tourist Track" to the summit (part of which is used in descent in Walk 40), but be well prepared for the Arctic weather conditions which may be encountered on the Ben at any time of year.

27. TYNDRUM to BRIDGE of ORCHY
a) over Beinn Odhar (901m)
b) via Auch Gleann and over Beinn Dorain (1074m)

SEE MAP G p108

ROUTE REVIEW

Stations:	Tyndrum Lower, Bridge of Orchy
Distance:	a) 12km (7½ miles); 630m ascent
	b) 20km (12½ miles); 970m ascent
Grade:	a) Difficult/Serious
	b) Serious
Map:	OS Landranger 50
Terrain:	a) involves steep descent over rough ground
	b) involves river crossings and the traverse of rugged and rocky mountain ridges and slopes
Estate:	Auch
Refreshments:	Bridge of Orchy Hotel

The route between Tyndrum and Bridge of Orchy Stations offers plenty of scope for mixing walks of different lengths and levels of difficulty. At the simplest there is the route which follows along the West Highland Way (see Walk 9); at the most challenging it is possible to take in two or more lofty and substantial mountains en route. The section of the Way from Tyndrum to Bridge of Orchy is not difficult (indeed until 1931 it constituted the old road to Glencoe) but offers rewarding views and the experience of walking on a sound track without route-finding problems albeit through lonely country.

Here we describe two alternatives:

The first involves the ascent of Beinn Odhar (dun-coloured hill) which, because of its relatively isolated position, is well-placed to offer excellent views on a clear day of most of the mountains of Argyll and Perthshire; the descent from it to Auch Gleann is rather steep and the route continues to Bridge of Orchy on the West Highland Way.

The second follows the West Highland Way to Auch and then proceeds up the lonely and steep-sided Auch Gleann to approach

Beinn Dorain (hill of the otter) from the NE. Beinn Dorain, a lofty Munro, which presents a daunting challenge from the S as it rises baldly to over 1000m, straddles a geological boundary, its lower slopes of Moine quartz mica schists being topped by Dalradian mica schists and limestone. The Gaelic poet Duncan Ban Macintyre, who lived in Auch Gleann for several years working as a herdsman for the Earl of Breadalbane, was inspired by Beinn Dorain to sing its praises in his *Final Farewell to the Bens*. This very long poem is a song about the passing of youth and the joyful way of life that ended when the glens emptied of people after the '45. One stanza, translated from the Gaelic, runs:

> And sweeter to my ear
> Is the concert of the deer
> In their roaring,
> Than when Erin from her Lyre
> Warmest strains of Celtic fire
> May be pouring.
> And no organ sends a roll
> So delightful to my soul
> As the branchy-crested race
> When they quicken their proud pace
> And bellow in the face
> Of Ben Dorain.

So, take your choice according to your fitness and energy level, and the prevailing weather - the mountains are lonely, and in parts trackless and the route over Ben Dorain is strenuous.

Tyndrum means "the house on the ridge", a reference to its proximity to the watershed nearby which separates the drainage of this part of Scotland; the River Fillan drains east from here through Strath Fillan while the River Lochy heads west through Glen Lochy. There are two stations at Tyndrum and it is Tyndrum Lower, on the Oban line which is the more convenient as the West Highland Way goes right past this station.

* * *

The West Highland Way follows along the right-hand side of the railway as it approaches Tyndrum Lower Station from

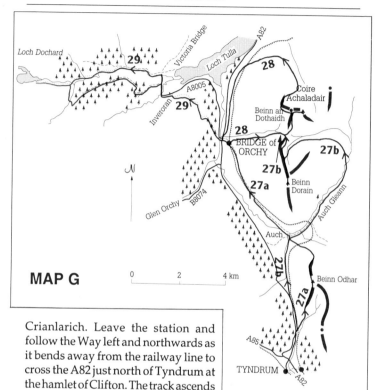

MAP G

Crianlarich. Leave the station and follow the Way left and northwards as it bends away from the railway line to cross the A82 just north of Tyndrum at the hamlet of Clifton. The track ascends alongside a burn, following the line of Major Caulfield's military road, built as part of a large network of military roads - seen as a means to pacify the eighteenth-century Jacobite risings. Prior to the new A82 trunk road being built, Caulfield's road became part of the old main road leading to Glencoe.

As you climb the track on its way through the the narrow incline with Beinn Odhar ahead and the shapely Beinn Dorain also coming into view, pause to look back across the head of Strath Fillan to the towering Beinn Dubhchraig ("black cliff"). Over the hills to the SW there is gold prospecting near Cononish. In earlier times there was lead mining in the area between Cononish and Clifton - lead was discovered in 1741 by Sir Robert Clifton

Ben Dorain and the West Highland Way

and worked until 1862. *The main vein extends northwards up the narrow glen you are walking through. The glen is probably a product of glacial action by a huge glacier from Rannoch Moor pushing southwards resulting in the very steep slopes on Ben Odhar, and as you go northwards, Beinn Dorain. Even today these slopes can be unstable and weathering can present a threat of landslide on to the adjacent railway line and, of course, the track of the West Highland Way.* About 1¹/₄km after crossing the A82 the Way crosses the railway over a bridge; here it's the line heading north to Fort William.

a) Over BEINN ODHAR

Strike off up the mossy hillside to your right, immediately after the railway bridge. An old track follows a somewhat indistinct ridge on the NW side of the Crom Allt for about ¹/₂km and then winds and zigzags up the hillside heading generally about N, (but with major deviations right and left of this), to reach a ruin associated with earlier lead mining activity, at a height of about 650m. From here continue up the hillside, still heading roughly N, fairly steeply at first then with the angle easing as the line converges with a fence coming up from the left to meet it at a fence junction near a small lochan. Continue on the same bearing up the steeper, boulder-strewn slope above and finally bear round to the left to reach the summit cairn and enjoy the views. *In the distance southwards are the Arrochar Alps (Walks in Part 1) and looking clockwise are Ben Lui (Walk 15), Ben Cruachan (Walk 22), the Black Mount peaks and Beinn Dorain.*

From the top of Beinn Odhar first head NNW and then pick your way down a steep slope covered with boulders, swinging round to the right (heading N) as the gradient eases. About 850 metres from the summit the slope steepens again to take up a convex form and you should take care. Head round further to the right at this point, roughly NE, and down an easier slope for about 500 metres, but, just before reaching the top of a crag, turn left and take a diagonal line downwards across the slope (heading WNW) to reach a footbridge over the railway.

At the hamlet of Auch the West Highland Line snakes around the famous Horse Shoe Curve and across a great viaduct. The area once had a royal hunting lodge, reputed to have been visited by James IV, and was a renowned deer forest, producing venison for the king.

From the bridge over the railway head towards the lovely old road bridge, of eighteenth-century segmented arch structure, and cross the river descending Auch Gleann. Continue N along the Way (still following Major Caulfield's military road) traversing beneath the steep slope of Beinn Dorain to cross over the railway as the valley widens out and the river you have been following turns SW into Glen Orchy. *There are extensive views down Glen Orchy but on the right the bulk of Beinn an Dothaidh (Walk 28) dominates separated from Beinn Dorain by the rugged Coire an Dothaidh at the head of the burn descending towards the Bridge of Orchy Station.*

It is easy walking on the Way to the station with ample scope to enjoy the views around. Bridge of Orchy itself comprises a few houses and the hotel, a stopping point for refreshment while awaiting the return train journey.

b) Via AUCH GLEANN and over BEINN DORAIN

The Way follows the railway along the W side of Beinn Odhar and descends gently to Auch - a diminutive meaning "the field of the hazel meadow". *At the end of the last century there was talk of putting a coach route eastwards through the glen to reach Glen Lyon but it remains today a wild and lonely place.*

From the hamlet of Auch do not cross the old bridge, but take the

Auch Gleann

track heading NE along the SE side of the Allt Kinglass, fording the Allt Coralan. The river is at first fringed by trees but after passing under the railway viaduct the glen is almost devoid of trees apart from plantations of pine and larch on the opposite hillside. Quite a contrast to the once thickly wooded deer forest in this area! Open views now prevail of the crags to the right on Beinn a'Chaisteil (883m) and the fine Coire Chruitein on the E side of Beinn Dorain. At 1074m the bulk of Beinn Dorain dominates, dropping steeply down into Auch from a bare, conical summit. It is best climbed from the col on its N side (between it and Beinn an Dothaidh) and our route continues round to there.

Just after a mature plantation on the NW side of the Allt Kinglass the track crosses the river via a ford but we can continue along the SE bank. The track recrosses ahead, after a burial ground and a young plantation on the NW side. Take an opportunity when possible to cross to the NW side before the sheep pens at Ais-an t-Sidhean; there is usually little water in the river here as most is diverted to a hydroelectric scheme at Loch Lyon. After crossing, head round the hillside ascending steadily to reach the Allt Coire a'Ghabhalach at about the point where it is dammed for the water take-off to Loch Lyon which will have been seen briefly to the E. (An alternative but longer route stays on the E side of the Allt Kinglass, crosses and recrosses the Allt a'Chuirn and then after crossing the Allt an Loin, follows the N side of the Allt Coire a'Ghabhalach.) Continue W alongside this burn along a level stretch to where a number of streams join, some 700 metres before and 120m below the col ahead.

For the summit of Beinn Dorain:

either follow up the stream which flows from the S, taking the tributary to the right in front of a large dark crag, and continue W to join the well-established path on the ridge leading S;

or continue up to the col (from which a descent can be made direct to Bridge of Orchy if desired) and then take the well-established path leading S.

From the col, or the burn junction, it is about 2km to the summit of Beinn Dorain; the path keeps on the ridge leading S to the summit and goes over a subsidiary top (about 1065m, with a cairn) before reaching the main summit (1074m) with its magnificent views.

To descend, retrace your steps to the col, keeping to the right, NE, near a small lochan - the ridge which continues N terminates in steep cliffs and should be avoided. From the col the path follows down to the W past some pointed boulders and zigzags down to cross the burn near a junction, then descending on the S side of the Allt Coire an Dothaidh. This route, wet and peaty in places, brings you down to Bridge of Orchy Station.

28. BEINN an DOTHAIDH (1002m) from BRIDGE of ORCHY

SEE MAP G p108

ROUTE REVIEW

Station:	Bridge of Orchy
Distance:	14km (9 miles); 810m ascent
Grade:	Serious
Map:	OS Landranger 50
Terrain:	steep mountain slopes and ridges, narrow and rocky in parts
Estate:	Blackmount (see Appendix B)
Refreshments:	Bridge of Orchy Hotel

Coire an Dothaidh from Bridge of Orchy Station

Bridge of Orchy marks the separation of the West Highland Way from the A82, and just a little further on at Achallader the railway line leaves the route of the A82 to strike off on its lonely course to Rannoch. Bridge of Orchy Station was the focus of a dispute which reached the House of Lords when the local landowner objected to the railway engineers' proposals to pipe a nearby burn to provide water (hardly a scarce resource!) at the station.

Towering up behind here are Beinn Dorain (Walk 27b) and Beinn an Dothaidh (pronounced "Ben an Doe", the mountain of scorching) on either side of Coire an Dothaidh. Here we describe the usual route up Beinn an Dothaidh from Bridge of Orchy via the col at the head of Coire an Dothaidh, but to provide an alternative descent we offer a route down into Coire Achaladair, (which requires careful navigation), returning from the NE end of Loch Tulla on the heathery slopes between the main road and the railway.

* * *

From the station take the underpass to the E side of the line, passing through a gate to follow a track which at first keeps left and then leads uphill on the S side of the Allt Coire an Dothaidh. This route, which can be somewhat wet and boggy, leads into a lower corrie where the path crosses one burn and continues E between this burn and another which is descending from the upper corrie on the left. The path now climbs fairly steeply, turning to the SE and passing pinnacle boulders which provide shelter in adverse weather, to the col at about 745m. (This is the route of descent in Walk 27b.)

From here turn left towards Beinn an Dothaidh, but the route then swings to the right of crags and heads about NE. Continue climbing, crossing a burn on the upper slopes of Coire a'Ghabhalach, and then turn to the N and more steeply onto the ridge above. This ridge leads via a cairn to the West Top, but the highest point is about $^1/2$km to the E. (A third top about 300 metres to the SE is lower.)

The route down into Coire Achaladair is not easy to find, and if the weather is not clear or you are not confident of your navigational abilities you should return by the route of ascent.

To proceed with the full route, return to the West Top and continue in the same direction downhill for about 600 metres, keeping to the left of some small cliffs. When the gradient reduces markedly turn to the right (NNE) and follow a minor path along a sharp ridge which drops away steeply on both sides. After about 800 metres the ridge, which has been bending towards the right, falls away steeply; turn to the right to descend slopes of heather and boulders into Coire Achaladair.

On reaching less steep and grassy slopes with many features characteristic of glacial moraines, turn NNW and continue downwards, parallel to the Allt Coire Achaladair but well above it; after about 1km turn further to the left, round the hillside but still losing height, to reach an underpass beneath the railway line at GR 308429. On the NW side of the line turn to the left, following the line of pylons to join a track (part of an old road) which leads past a large cairn. *This commemorates the bond of allegiance between the Fletchers of Achallader and the Stewarts of Appin at the time of the Battle of Legando in 1468.* The track leads down to the A82 about 1km beyond the cairn, but the traffic can be largely avoided by continuing on the rough ground for a further $1^1/2$km until you have almost reached the Bridge of Orchy Hotel and road junction, and then taking to the main road.

29. VICTORIA BRIDGE and LOCH DOCHARD from BRIDGE of ORCHY

SEE MAP G p108

ROUTE REVIEW

Station:	**Bridge of Orchy**
Distance:	**23km (14¹/₂ miles); 280m ascent**
Grade:	**Moderate**
Map:	**OS Landranger 50**
Terrain:	**mostly tracks and paths, muddy in places**
Estates:	**Blackmount; Glenkinglass**
Refreshments:	**Bridge of Orchy Hotel; Inveroran Hotel**

Bridge of Orchy Station is on the West Highland Way as it leads northwards en route to Kingshouse (see Walk 30). The Hotel at Bridge of Orchy seems to have been established relatively recently (compared with that at Inveroran, see below); old postcards from about 1910 show no hotel in the location; however its establishment, and rebuilding around 1960 after fire, has been welcomed by many travellers, not least a considerable number who found themselves marooned there between 21st and 25th January 1984 when the A82 was snowbound.

The area has many historical and literary connections. The Inn at Inveroran was established around 1707 (vying with Kingshouse for the title "oldest inn in Scotland"!) on a well used drovers' route to Falkirk from the west; there was once a cattle stance here but the Marquis of Breadalbane sought to close it, establishing a replacement at Tyndrum. The drovers however objected that this was too far. The dispute was finally resolved by the siting of a new stance at Achallader. Inveroran boasted the Wordsworths and Robert Southey amongst its more illustrious visitors in the early nineteenth century. Less well known perhaps was the innkeeper's daughter, Mary Ban (Fair Mary); the Gaelic bard, Duncan Ban Macintyre, who was born in a nearby croft, Druimliart, the ruins of which can still be seen, fell in love with and married her. (Note: there is a monument to him which is a focal point of another walk (17b) from Dalmally Station [see p77].)

*   *   *

Our route follows the indicated West Highland Way (WHW) across the A82 below the station and takes the signed A8005 (a mere single track road with passing places which is an option for the return route), to cross the humped-back Bridge of Orchy itself (an Ancient Monument dating back to about 1742).

The road bends sharp right immediately after the bridge but the WHW is signed straight ahead leading up a rough path, perhaps muddy at first through forest plantation. *The Way is an attractive route over Mam Carraigh, following the general line of the military road built in the 1750s. The highest point of this route affords excellent views of the peaks to the N and W of Loch Dochard, particularly the fine corrie of Stob Ghabhar, and NE across Loch Tulla. The lochside property and surrounding estate, once the property of the Marquis of Breadalbane, is now owned by the family of the late Ian Fleming, creator of James Bond; Major Philip Fleming had an interest in restoring the Caledonian Pine Forest, remnants of which grace the shores of Loch Tulla.*

The Way descends easily down to the small hotel at Inveroran; from here, follow the road round to its end at Victoria Bridge, *so called because Queen Victoria stayed near here in the nineteenth century in her search for a Highland residence. In winter and spring you may be fortunate enough to see deer in the pines around the flats at the edge of Loch Tulla.*

A hundred metres or so from the bridge turn left in front of a cottage (Forest Lodge) along a track signposted Glen Etive via Glen Kinglass (through Clashgour Estate). Take this rough stony track which follows the river bank on the N side of the Abhainn Shira and offers good views ahead and right. On the right-hand side is Clashgour Hut. *Once a tiny schoolhouse, the hut is now leased to the University of Glasgow Mountaineering Club by the estate on the understanding that users check and respect the stalking requirements during August and September which seems a healthy acknowledgement of varying usage of the hills.*

In about 200 metres there is a gate and stile across the track at which point you turn off left to take a small footpath between the forestry fence and the river. After some 2km you reach a small footbridge alongside a ford over a tributary of the main river. Continue over the bridge (or brave the ford!) along a double track for a short way and on reaching the main river bank turn right along a narrow path (rather than across another ford which spans the river ahead at that point). Some ¹/₂km further on the path reaches a river crossing via a nicely proportioned if somewhat dilapidated suspension bridge (take care!).

Beyond here the track turns right to Loch Dochard and Glen Kinglass and although you can omit the 2km each way to the Loch, its splendid solitude and setting makes it worth the continuation. *Wainwright was struck here by "the profound silence and absence of movement (adding to) the impressiveness of the scene".* Retrace your steps to the suspension bridge but, instead of re-crossing it, head S up over a rough tussocky slope for about ¹/₂km keeping to the right of the Allt Suilna Curra (the burn which descends towards a stand of fine pines on your left). There is a bridge over the tumbling water and a stile in the fence beyond. (The banks of the burn just above the bridge offer a good spot for rest or refreshment.) Cross these and then strike uphill for about 150 metres alongside the fence to a firebreak which leads leftwards on to a forest road network.

Follow the forest road E for about 2¹/₂km, passing through two gates to a T-junction. Turn right and uphill, then swing left as the forest track resumes an easterly direction and passes close to the ruins of Druimliart, continuing through further gates to return to the A8005 just S of Victoria Bridge. Retrace your steps to Inveroran where you have a choice of either following the road along the shore of Loch Tulla and through the ancient pine forest of Doire Darach - perhaps the quietest A-road in the U.K. - or taking the West Highland Way route back again, not least for the superb views east of Beinn Achaladair, Beinn an Dothaidh (Walk 28), Beinn Dorain and Beinn Odhar (Walks 27a and b) and beyond.

An INTRODUCTION to RANNOCH MOOR

The area between Bridge of Orchy and Corrour includes renowned Rannoch Moor with a magic all of its own.

> Yea, a desert wide and wasted,
> Washed by rainfloods to the bones
> League on league of heather blasted
> Storm-gnashed moss, grey boulder stones.
> *(Principal Shairp, Prof of Poetry at Oxford)*

The name "Rannoch" has two possible derivations: from the Gaelic "ruineach" meaning bracken, or, more likely, from "ratheanach" meaning watery.

Set at over 300m above sea level, it comprises a tableland or amphitheatre floored by weak granite, some 400 million years old; this is overlaid by blanket bog, strewn with boulders, and surrounded by majestic ranks of hills which have been more resistant to erosion. This was an area of great ice accumulation during the period of the Pleistocene Glaciation and the pattern of radial ice dispersal from it is evident in the U-shaped valleys through the surrounding mountains. While predominantly bog and with numerous lochs and lochans, there is discernable drainage via the river which barely saunters down the merest of gradients from Loch Ba to Loch Laidon.

Rannoch Moor has been variously described (and in more positive vein than above!); *Mountain, Moor and Loch*, written in 1895 to describe the country through which the new West Highland Railway would run, depicts Rannoch Moor in winter as a "study in sepia" and in summer as "one colossal turkey carpet so rich and oriental is the colouring". Tom Weir has detailed some of its life - bobbing wheatears and dunlin, the lochs fringed by bog bean, cotton grass and bog myrtle; it even sports a unique Rannoch Rush, some 12 inches high with a six petalled yellow/green flower. However it featured in classical literature as "a wearier desert man never saw" (R.L.Stevenson).

Bridge of Orchy

In Roman times the moor was forested and as recently as the mid eighteenth century it supported a fairly large population of some 2,500 people but by the mid 1980s the numbers had dwindled to around 400. The Rannoch Clearances saw evictions (documented by Alexander Mackenzie in 1883), many brought about by deteriorating economic conditions. Black-faced sheep replaced cattle but a fall in wool prices ensued which, together with food shortages, led to a decline in crofting. The moors saw the advent of grouse shooting and deer stalking and Scottish Lairds were supplanted by new landowners, notably the Forestry Commission and latterly Germans, Italians and Dutch. There has been intermittent influx of people on the moor, in particular those engaged in building the West Highland Railway at the end of the nineteenth century and those constructing the dam for the Blackwater Reservoir early in the twentieth century and the new Glencoe road in the 1930s. The eighteenth century saw soldiers billeted after the '45 Jacobite uprising in barracks at the west end of Loch Rannoch for whom the "Soldiers Trenches" (an attempt to drain shieling land) were devised in the hope of giving them work useful to the local community.

More detail is available in A.D.Cunningham's book, *The History of Rannoch*.

Legends and folk-tales about the region are many and have been compiled in an enchanting book, *Tales of Rannoch*, also by A.D.Cunningham, published in 1989. As the population waned so, earlier, had the trees: the demise of Rannoch forest we should perhaps lay at the door of two jealous giants, Anier and Anear, whose confrontations over the watersheds on the moor led them to tear up the trees, using the trunks as clubs and missiles. It took some 30 days for them to render the moor into the treeless wilderness it appears today but the stumps of the Scots pines which cloaked the moor some 6000 years ago can still be seen preserved in the peat - such wood is said to have torch-like properties when set alight. There are those who maintain more prosaically that the trees were felled for firewood, building crofts and ships, and for making charcoal for iron smelting in the bloomeries but the reader must make his choice between these "histories"!

The Formorians, two giants living in the Black Corries of Rannoch Moor, were further responsible for the landscape we see today. They were forever arguing about their strength when a wise Young Man from Rannoch set them a task to settle the quarrel, suggesting that the stronger was the one who could throw a stone the farthest. They vainly and eagerly embarked on the contest, more and more stones, larger and larger boulders scattering the moor, the greatest travelling as far as Bridge of Gaur and beyond. (There is also a story about a giant ice sheet which moved across the moor some 20,000 years ago tearing rocks away along its path and dropping them again - for more detail of this we refer you to the Introduction.) Many stories are associated with particular boulders, evoked by their shapes or markings; some have the letter M inscribed to show the boundary of the Menzies lands, a major estate in the Rannoch area.

Rannoch Moor has inspired both writers (of fact and whimsy) and artists, as well as those concerned to research its history, geology, flora and fauna and those interested in learning more about this fascinating region will find some pointers in the bibliography at the end of this book. As far as the walker is concerned this is not an area to trifle with. Not only is it remote with great distances between stations and habitation but its legacy of poor drainage, due to both geology and glacial history, has led to instances of people getting lost or stuck in peat bogs. It is not difficult to sink to the thighs or further, a serious plight and potentially lethal for the solo walker. These hazards had great implications for the construction of the railway which ultimately (after much trial and error, in the form of sunken material lost to sight and consequently swallowed money!) was "floated" across on layered rafts of turf and brushwood, a bedding which still forms its "foundation" today.

Exploration prior to the construction also had its moments; in January 1889 a party of seven gentlemen, including Sir Robert MacAlpine, engaged in prospecting the route across Rannoch Moor, set off on what has become a notorious expedition. Ill clad and sporting umbrellas they were to embark on a crossing of the moor in the depths of winter, starting by crossing Loch Treig in a rowing boat. Disaster upon disaster subsequently befell them; they spent much of the time jumping from tussock to tussock to keep out of the bog; one of the party collapsed and became unconscious, his only shelter a makeshift umbrella-tent. Another set off alone to make for Gorton, miraculously stumbling over a fence, and stunning himself in the process, but then managing to follow it to his destination. A rescue was effected and the party eventually reunited near Inveroran just in time to escape the onset of a severe blizzard. (John Thomas has a graphic account of this epic in his classic book *The West Highland Railway*).

As far as possible our routes follow established tracks but there are some sections of hard going over peat bogs without track. Make sure that if you venture across the Moor (Walks 30ii, 31 and 32) you are well prepared and if possible choose clear settled weather after a good dry spell (or during a hard frost, but days may then be somewhat short for the distances involved).

30. BRIDGE of ORCHY to RANNOCH via KINGSHOUSE

SEE MAP H p123

ROUTE REVIEW

Stations:	Bridge of Orchy, Rannoch
Distance:	i) Bridge of Orchy to Kingshouse 19km (12 miles); 560m ascent
	ii) Kingshouse to Rannoch 19km (12 miles); 160m ascent
Grade:	i) Moderate
	ii) Difficult
Maps:	OS Landrangers 41, 42 and 50
Terrain:	mostly good tracks and paths with some rougher going in the middle of the second part. NB. Very remote country, with no shelter or habitation over long distances
Estates:	Blackmount; Rannoch Deer Management Association; Black Corries (see Appendix B)
Refreshments:	Inveroran Hotel; Kingshouse Hotel; Rannoch - Station Tearoom; Moor of Rannoch Hotel

The full flavour of remote and wild Rannoch Moor is on offer on this long route from Bridge of Orchy to Kingshouse, and on to Rannoch. You will probably want to spend two days over the 38km, but there is accommodation available at historic Kingshouse, a hotel conveniently situated at the midway point. The route across Black Mount (in the Highlands "mount" or "mounth" refers not so much to a hill as to a high plateau) to Glencoe has a long history. Originally a drove road, for centuries it was the main route from NW Scotland to the cattle fairs or "trysts" at Crieff, and then from 1770 at Falkirk, and was tramped by some 10,000 black Highland cattle, with perhaps three times as many sheep annually. A military road was constructed around 1750 by General Wade's successor and Inspector of Roads, Major Caulfield who allegedly penned the lines:

"If you'd seen these roads before they were made,
You'd lift up your hands and bless General Wade."

The nineteenth-century "main" road to Glencoe also used much of these original drove and military road routes before the present A82 was constructed in the 1930s. The old route was taken for some 60 years by a coach service from Glasgow to Fort William dating from 1843 and must have been quite some journey.

* * *

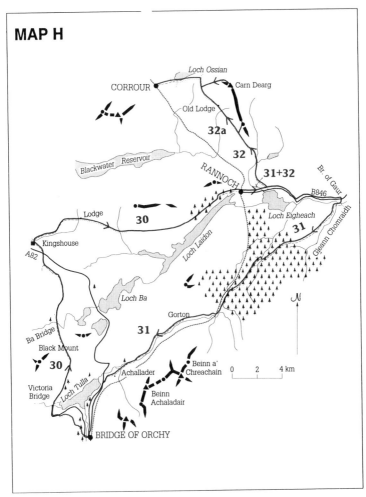

MAP H

Loch Ossian

CORROUR

Carn Dearg

Old Lodge

32a

32

Blackwater Reservoir

RANNOCH

31+32

Br. of Gaur

B846

Lodge

30

Loch Eigheach

31

Kingshouse

A82

Loch Laidon

Gleann Chomraich

Loch Ba

Gorton

N

31

Ba Bridge

Black Mount

30

Achallader

Beinn a' Chreachain

0   2   4 km

Victoria Bridge

Loch Tulla

Beinn Achaladair

BRIDGE OF ORCHY

i) Bridge of Orchy to Kingshouse

The route from Bridge of Orchy Station to Victoria Bridge is described in Walk 29 (Map G) and you should follow this taking the West Highland Way over Mam Carraigh or take the quiet A8005 which follows around the shoreline of Loch Tulla. At Victoria Bridge continue on to the end of the public road where several routes radiate from Forest Lodge.

Our route from here follows the West Highland Way - look for the thistle symbol - taking the old Glencoe road (on a parallel line to the military road which is slightly higher up the hill) and ascends gently alongside the woods of Black Mount, over cobbles compacted by booted bipeds and cloven quadrupeds. This is still a service road for cattle and sometimes a landrover may be seen dishing out animal fodder.

After the wooded area the surroundings open out, the Way reaching a high point at 320m where there is a vista across Loch Tulla. However it is shortly the expanse of Rannoch Moor which grips the attention. *Drumlins, upturned scoops of glacial deposit, abound and the lochans to your right contrast with the peaks and corries, notably Coire Ba, said to be the largest corrie in Scotland, to the left of the track. The relics of the Ice Age are all around, reminders of the ice sheet that covered Rannoch Moor. This is deer "forest" country par excellence and if you are lucky you may hear the roar of the rutting red deer stags in autumn or see some young calves with hinds in spring. Originally the deer were forest inhabitants but as the forest vanished they adapted to the new habitat; the term "deer forest" has been retained, albeit something of a misnomer.*

Caulfield's old military road and the Way join up and continue on to Ba Bridge (dating from the early nineteenth century, the era of Thomas Telford who instituted improvements along this route), which crosses a rocky mini-gorge forged by the River Ba en route to the flat expanse of the Moor. About 1km further on the ruins of Ba Cottage are reached, *a one-time crofters home, perhaps abandoned with the Clearances during the great demise of the rural population of Scotland. Alongside the path near the cottage is a mound suggesting evidence of a grave in the Highland traditional burial system. Some 2km beyond the cottage, near the highest point on this section of the Way, is a cairn to Peter Fleming, brother of Ian Fleming, who had a colourful career as a special correspondent for The Times. He died of a heart attack while shooting near*

Buachaille Etive Mor

this spot in August 1971.

The Way now skirts around the shoulder of Meall a'Bhuiridh towards the head of the superb Glencoe valley. *On the northern slopes of the mountain is the White Corries ski-lift, developed in the 1950s and 1960s by Scotland's first commercial ski company; recent improvements and additions here include a restaurant. The near distance is dominated by the towering bulk of Buachaille Etive Mor, the* "great shepherd of Etive", *which offers fine climbing, and scrambling in summer.* At the junction with the road to the ski-lift sits Blackrock Cottage, its roof well secured by hanging rocks; it is "home" to the Ladies Scottish Climbing Club. Continue on here to cross the A82 at an angle where a track leads ahead to Kingshouse Hotel, (once a cattle "stance" on the droving route from the west, which claims (perhaps among others!) to be the oldest inn in Scotland. *Its remoteness led to the landlord in the eighteenth century living rent free as an incentive to stay though apparently participation in illegal salt smuggling was a lucrative sideline. It undoubtedly has a long history, once used as a barracks for the troups of George III after Culloden (1745), hence the name "Kings House". Dorothy Wordsworth in 1803 described the place "as dirty as a house after a sale on a rainy day" and chronicled the poor food, damp and bare rooms in her journal.Today all that has changed and you should find a warm welcome but book ahead, for there is no other accommodation in this lonely spot.*

ii) Kingshouse to Rannoch

The walk from Kingshouse to Rannoch "is not recommended unless you have plenty of time, a compass, a watch and a good sense of direction, and should on no account be attempted except in the best of weather". Thus warned Michael Pollard in *Walking the Scottish Highlands* as recently as 1984. Perhaps a little on the dire side, but the walker indeed needs to be quite self-sufficient and competent so as not to join the ranks of four skeletons allegedly found on the Moor during a police search for a missing person! Legend has it however that "An Duine Mor" (the Great Man) appears whenever people are lost, apparently leading them onto the track before disappearing.

Our route follows a good track as far as Black Corries but this deteriorates as you proceed beyond until you join a forest road above Loch Laidon, some 3km before reaching Rannoch Station.

*   *   *

From Kingshouse cross the bridge immediately N of the Hotel and turn right at the T-junction in 200 metres to follow the well-maintained gravel road alongside the river. Passing a communications tower at GR 278545 and a forestry plantation on the right opposite a deeply incised burn, the track proceeds towards Black Corries Lodge, a shooting lodge with various outbuildings, located in a fenced enclosure surrounded by some mixed woodland. Here the footpath is diverted around the N side of the policies, and there are good views from the higher ground of the area you are to traverse ahead. Avoid the left turn about 250 metres after the diversion and continue on to reach another communications tower at GR 314555. A better track leads to the tower but ours continues on over grass and heather past a lochan on the right. Overhead power lines come in from the left and the track makes a sharp left turn at a bridge. After about 1km the track terminates at a small cairn.

There are two routes ahead; take the left-hand one, keeping up and parallel to the overhead lines. A path converges with these after about 1km. After a further 1/2km cross an electric fence at a stile and continue under the power lines. Cross the Allt Riabhach na Bioraich above the ruins of Tigh na Cruaiche; after this the path widens with evidence of use by all-terrain vehicles (ATV) and, as the forest comes into sight, it descends and then, after a ruined enclosure, climbs again to enter the forest at a gate and stile. The ATV tracks undulate through a break in the forest beneath the power lines and after about $1^3/_4$km they leave the power lines and go steeply uphill to the end of the forest road just before a burn. Follow this first up and then down, rejoining the power lines before emerging from the forest after about $1^3/_4$km at a gate and stile. Here you join a lower road which has come from a launching point on Loch Laidon. The gravel road follows alongside a sandy beach and in 1km reaches the level crossing at the station, another remote outpost situated some 300 metres above sea level, with a hotel, the Moor of Rannoch and the Station Tearoom, operated in summer by the McLellans, the family of the last station master there.

31. RANNOCH to BRIDGE of ORCHY via BRIDGE of GAUR

SEE MAP H p123

ROUTE REVIEW

Stations:	Rannoch, Bridge of Orchy
Distance:	39km (24½ miles) but see NB below; 140m ascent
Grade:	Difficult (but see warning under Terrain)
Map:	OS Landranger 50 & 51
Terrain:	mainly good forest and farm tracks, but some rough ground including 1km of potentially treacherous bog over the watershed; also fords. Do not attempt after wet weather or when burns are in spate
Estate:	Lochs; Blackmount (see Appendix B)
Refreshments:	Bridge of Orchy Hotel; (nothing between stations)

NB. The distance can be reduced by 8km by using the Post Bus to Bridge of Gaur

This is a long route in very remote country through Rannoch Forest and over Rannoch Moor and you should heed the warning under "Terrain". There is an ancient right of way from Bridge of Gaur to Achallader which kept on higher ground over the watershed, but recent forestry plantation has made part of this route impracticable and it is now best to use the forest roads as far as possible. You might consider carrying spare footwear so that you have something dry to wear along the track from Gorton.

In following this route from east to west you can take advantage of the Post Bus service from Rannoch (where it is scheduled to meet the morning train from Glasgow) to Bridge of Gaur. You will also find the views better going in this direction. This route traverses classic Rannoch Moor: bog, solitude or isolation (depending on your point of view!), with superb surrounding mountain scenery; it is also a walk interspersed with some history and legend.

* * *

Either walk E along the road to Bridge of Gaur or take the Post Bus, which goes from Rannoch Station to Pitlochry, through boulder-strewn country and past the power station below Loch Eigheach. According to the day of the week the bus will drop you **either** at the junction of the road round the S side of Loch Rannoch and the B846 **or** at the bridge itself 400m to the S.

The house next to the bridge, Tigh na Linn, was once an inn and on one notable occasion a stopping place for a funeral party carrying a Macgregor clansman through Bridge of Gaur to Balquidder and in need of some refreshment. They rested and imbibed in the parlour so well that they omitted to take the coffin with them on their departure. So enraged was Lady Menzies, the landowner, that she closed down the inn forthwith and Bridge of Gaur has since lacked any hostelry. The old manse at Bridge of Gaur was once the home of Rev A.E.Robertson, minister at the Braes of Rannoch Church for 11 years, and the first person to complete the ascent of all the Munros (in 1901).

Turn right immediately over the bridge to Invercomrie Deer Farm between a cottage on the left and a fine house known as Rannoch Barracks, built near the site of the soldiers' barracks established in 1746 after the Battle of Culloden, on the right. There are high deer fences, but gates allow you through; keep left in front of the farm and follow the track up between heather and boulders (this is the steepest climb of the day!). About 800 metres beyond the farm a track joins from the left, and you emerge into a broad, fairly level valley, Gleann Chomraidh. To the S you will see Meall Buidhe (932m) and in the distance to the SW you will briefly see the mountains above Achallader; Bridge of Orchy lies beyond these!

Strathossian (34)
An Dubh Lochan, near Fersit (35)

At the head of Loch Treig (36)
C.I.C. Hut (40)

The track takes you easily up the glen, past a ruin on the left, and then through a gate into new forestry plantation. Before the trees ahead obscure them, you will get views along part of this track to the hills of the Black Mount. About 5km after leaving the road the track enters the mature forest, and it is as though you are entering a different enclosed world. In this part of the forest the trees are thickly planted, mainly pines, and there has been wind damage adding to the inpenetrability. Smaller tracks lead off to the left and then right, but continue ahead for about 2km; here a less-used green track goes ahead and provides the shorter route, but it involves a ford crossing, and if you are wanting to keep your feet dry at this stage of the walk you will prefer to turn right and follow the main track over a bridge and then to the left.

About 1km beyond the bridge the track from the ford rejoins the main track, and in a further 400 metres there is a small cairn on the right, marking a path to the Soldiers Trenches, and shortly afterwards an open grassy area on the left. After a little over 1km the track emerges into a relatively open area with smaller trees and the views of the mountains ahead can again be appreciated.

In due course you will reach a line of pylons, about 200 metres from where the railway passes over a river; there is a wind generator here providing power for electric fences around the forest - bear this in mind when you come to cross them! Leave the track here and turn to the left following all-terrain vehicle tracks over rough ground along the line of the pylons for about 1$^{1/}$4km; there are two burns to be forded along here. This will bring you to a gate at the end of the forest with a high stile alongside.

Once over the fence you reach the treacherous part of this route - about 1km of bog and peat hags across the watershed between drainage to Loch Rannoch and the east and that to Loch Tulla and the west.

It is here that the railway construction involved a "flotation" across the morass of bog. Layers upon layers of turf and brushwood, followed by soil and ash were swallowed up by bog until eventually the springy carpet held up and formed an elongated raft to support the line. A director of the line, a Mr Renton, bailed out the dire finances of this expensive construction and in tribute to him the navvies sculpted a stone head of Renton, to be seen on Rannoch Station platform.

So, BEWARE: there are frightening stories of people disappearing up to their armpits and further in bogs on Rannoch Moor.

The alternative strategies across here seem to be to keep to the left where, after a little way, you will find the bank of the Allt Coire a'Bhuic provides firmer ground, or to opt for the security given by the fence along the railway to the right. In either case you will reach the point where the tributaries joining together to form the Water of Tulla pass under the railway at GR 399484 (almost exactly at the junction of OS Landranger Maps 50 and 51), providing the opportunity for you also to pass under the railway on the right side of the river.

Continue for about 2½km along the right bank of this delightful river as it winds through its valley cut into glacial debris. The easiest walking is usually immediately alongside the river and the temptation to cut corners will lead into boggy and tussocky ground. At GR 379481 a bridge is shown on the OS map over the Water of Tulla, but in 1993 this was down perhaps having been destroyed sometime earlier by floods. From here head uphill a little, still on the right of the river, to Gorton Bothy which is well hidden behind a small knoll. This is maintained by the Scottish Mountain Bothies Association and will provide some shelter for a stop if the weather is unkind.

There was once a private station on the West Highland Line near here, together with housing for railway personnel, minders for the trains as they passed over Rannoch Moor. Originally a passing place for trains, for a period Gorton boasted a school in an old railway carriage with as many as eleven pupils.

From Gorton bothy a good track leads down to Achallader, going over or round the numerous hummocks of glacial deposits. *There are superb views along here of the mountains on the left, Beinn Chreachain and Beinn Achaladair, and later Beinn an Dothaidh (Walk 28) and of their N facing corries created by glacial erosion; beneath them is the ancient Crannach Forest with fine Caledonian pines and deciduous trees. You may ponder on the contrast between a forest such as this created by nature and that which you passed through earlier planted by man.*

Towards the ruined house of Barravourich, Loch Tulla comes into view and you enter enclosed pasture on the flood plain of the

Across Loch Tulla, S end, from Walks 28 and 31

Water of Tulla and then cross the bridge to the S side of the river. You will now get closer views of the hills of the Black Mount - Stob a'Choire Odhair, Clach Leathad and Meall a'Bhuiridh. There is still one more obstacle to negotiate before you reach Achallader Farm: the track fords the Allt Coire Achaladair.

The old tower here is a relic of Achallader Castle, one time stonghold of the Fletchers; it was from here that the Campbells of Glen Lyon set out to confront the Macdonalds in Glencoe resulting in the notorious massacre. The area became used as a droving stance, replacing that at Inveroran (Walk 29). Beyond the farm the track continues to join the main A82 road in just over 1km. Bridge of Orchy is still about 4¹/₂km away, but there are alternatives to the main road on the left. It is possible to take to the hillside before joining the main road, but as there is a new plantation to be negotiated shortly after the junction it is probably best to follow the road for about ¹/₂km, and take to the hillside beyond it. A track, which can be reached from a gate by the road shortly after an old milestone, winds beneath the line of pylons between the road and railway for about 1¹/₂km, passing the ruins of a large old cairn (see Walk 28). When the track returns to the road it is still fairly easy to stay on the rough ground, perhaps following what appear to be the foundations of an old military road, returning to the main road only 100 metres or so before the Bridge of Orchy Hotel and the minor road leading up to the station.

32. RANNOCH to CORROUR
a) via Corrour Old Lodge
b) via Carn Dearg (941m)

SEE MAP H p123

ROUTE REVIEW

Stations:	Rannoch, Corrour
Distance:	a) 18km (11 miles); 200m ascent
	b) 20km (12½ miles); 670m ascent
Grade:	a) Moderate
	b) Difficult/Serious
Maps:	OS Landranger 41 & 42
Terrain:	a) mountain tracks and paths
	b) mountain slopes and ridges - fairly easy-angled and heathery
Estates:	Dunan; Corrour (see Appendix B)
Refreshments:	at Rannoch only - Station Tearoom; Moor of Rannoch Hotel

These walks can be done in either direction, and by starting at Corrour there are the advantages of starting more than 100m above the finish and having a hotel and tearoom at the end, but this is "The Road to the Isles" and for the romantic, humming "by Loch Tummel and Loch Rannoch and Lochaber I will go" it must surely be done heading towards the Isles! This is the direction we follow and we describe two alternatives here: the first a fairly low level route remaining on The Road to the Isles; the second, for the more energetic and intrepid, follows an inviting ridge to the "Munro" summit of Carn Dearg (pronounced 'carn jerrak', the red hill). The two alternatives follow a common route for 8km and rejoin before descending along The Road to the Isles to Loch Ossian.

*   *   *

From Rannoch Station set off E along the (only) road, across the moor. An old ruin is passed on the left and the road crosses the Allt Eigheach flowing into Loch Eigheach on the right. The road leads on ahead with pylons "marching" alongside towards Schiehallion (1083m), with its characteristic pointed shape when viewed from this side; about 400 metres after the bridge (and 2½km from the station), however, our route turns sharply left. There is a Scottish Rights Of Way Society signpost telling us that this is "The Road to the Isles" leading to Fort William by Corrour, but this is placed to be seen when approaching from the other side.

Alongside this junction is a large, heart-shaped boulder known as the "broken heart stone". In its original location, where the old Road to the Isles approached Loch Eigheach, the then complete boulder afforded shelter to travellers; however, those building an earlier road over the moor found it blocking their route and in attempting to move it split it into its present shape, hence its name. The stone then came under threat of submergence by the construction of the Gaur Hydro-Electric scheme whereupon the people of Rannoch persuaded the contractors to move the stone to its present position where today's travellers can rest en route to the Isles.

A gate about 100 metres along the track ensures that it is not used by unauthorised vehicles. There are now views back across Rannoch Moor to the mountains of Glencoe and the Black Mount, and further left to those E of Bridge of Orchy.

The track climbs steadily, and in the ditches draining the moor on either side old roots have been exposed providing testimony to the widespread trees once present here and used for charcoal in the fifteenth-century local iron-smelting hearths. Hills come into view ahead, but these are easy-angled and give the feel of extensive wild country rather than spectacular mountains. The track swings round to the right, away from the railway, and, after fording the Allt Gormag (which can usually be crossed fairly easily on boulders unless it is in spate), brings us to a bridge back over the Allt Eigheach. On the other side continue N alongside the burn until after about 600 metres the path turns sharply left. As the path continues to ascend, the slopes become heathery and the Blackwater Reservoir comes into view on the left. *This reservoir was created by the building of a huge dam between 1905 and 1909 by up to 3000 navvies to provide water to drive the turbines in the power house of the aluminium works at Kinlochleven.*

a) via Corrour Old Lodge - The Road to the Isles (low level route)

The path reaches a height of 550m along the side of Sron Leachd a'Chaorainn, and then descends to the ruins of Corrour Old Lodge. *Positioned on the Road to the Isles, in its heyday the Lodge, at 525m above sea level, claimed to be the highest shooting lodge in Scotland; with the coming of the railway it was replaced by the new Corrour Lodge at the end of Loch Ossian and the Old Lodge became used as an isolation hospital for a while and it is difficult to imagine a more isolated spot! Eventually it fell into disuse and the roof was stripped off to save the need to pay rates on the building.*

After this the path rises a little, still traversing the hillside now below the W ridge of Carn Dearg from where route b) descends.

b) via Carn Dearg (941m)

On a clear day and for those with time and energy, the ridge from Sron Leachd a'Chaorainn to Carn Dearg (about 3km in length) provides a fine high level traverse. It is best to continue on the track for at least 1¹/₂km after the sharp left turn away from the Allt Eigheach before heading up the slope on the right to gain the S end of the ridge. The ridge itself is broad and undulating with lochans in two of the cols at the S end. There is steep ground on the right, however, so do not stray in that direction. The ascent of about 110m from the final col to the summit is quite steep and swings round left to the NW. The views from here are splendid in all directions.

To descend continue NW for about 400 metres to a small knoll, and then, instead of following this ridge further, head down left (W) to the broad easy W ridge. Loch Ossian comes into sight below on the right. In about 1km the angle steepens and the ground becomes tussocky, but continue in the same general direction to rejoin The Road to the Isles at about the point where it begins its descent towards Loch Ossian.

Keep left at a fork where there is a granite boulder on the left-hand side; facing Loch Ossian there is a plaque here in memory of a young man who drowned in the loch in March 1979. Follow the path which continues downhill to the head of Loch Ossian. Directly ahead in the distance will be seen the distinctive cone shape of Binnein Beag with further peaks in the Mamores range to its left; to its right are the peaks of Ben Nevis and the Grey Corries which provide an increasingly impressive backdrop as you approach Corrour Station.

Traversing the shoulder of Meall na Lice above you to the left spare a thought for earlier travellers on this stretch of the Road to the

Isles. There is a tale of a couple with a mare en route from Rannoch who were caught by a severe storm; already exhausted and now soaked to the skin the wife collapsed. The husband, fearing that she would not survive while he fetched help from their destination at Loch Treig, knocked down the mare and disembowelled it to provide a warm cavity in which to shelter his wife who thus survived the elements. You will see the Mare's Stone where this incident occurred at GR 377670.

Join the track which has come along the S shore of Loch Ossian (Walk 33), shortly before passing the youth hostel at the head of the loch, and continue on to reach the station in a further 1³/₄km.

33. AROUND LOCH OSSIAN from CORROUR

SEE MAP I p136

ROUTE REVIEW

Station:	Corrour
Distance:	14km (8½ miles); 20m ascent
Grade:	Easy (but see NB below)
Map:	OS Landranger 41 & 42
Terrain:	very good clear track with some high stiles to cross
Estate:	Corrour
Refreshments:	None at all

NB. It is very important to be completely self-sufficient in this remote area and remember you are about 400m above sea level!

Corrour Station, situated at 400m (over 1300 feet) above sea level and the highest in the British Isles, gives access to a magical area within Rannoch Moor. Loch Ossian is the focal point and can be reached only by rail and foot - there are no public roads here - and on this easy walk around the loch you can savour the views in peace and tranquillity. If this is not enough then you can always try the real challenge here to "Run around Loch Ossian in under an Hour", a feat perpetuated by Tom Rigg, for many years warden of the simple SYHA hostel on the shore of the loch. Tom has "Club" records of the successful contenders since the run began in 1977, with a shield commemorating the 500th achievement in July 1991. With five out of every six contestants failing to beat the clock around

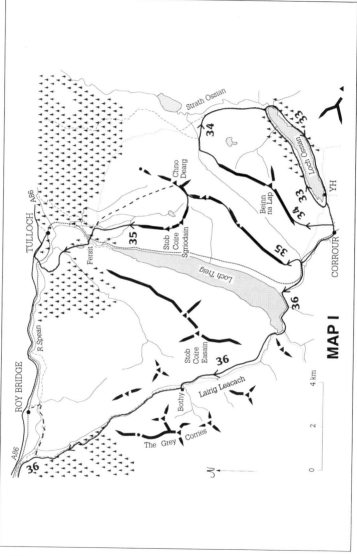

MAP I

the 12km (7½ miles), no fewer than 24 different nationalities have succeeded in the attempt. There is a challenge to pensioners to pip Tom's intended achievement when he reaches the age of 65 in March 1995! Tom has also tamed some of the local inhabitants such that a couple of red deer stags will come and feed from his hand. Perhaps you will be fortunate to see some nearby.

*   *   *

When you can tear yourself away from the views from the station platform, turn down the track eastwards towards Loch Ossian. The impressive mountains in the distance are Aonach Beag and the remote Ben Alder. After about 1km turn left at the crossroads to follow the track round the N side of the loch, skirting the foot of Beinn na Lap (Walk 34). The track crosses the lower slopes of the mountain before entering the forest, a mixture of old and new plantation together with some old pines. *If you are lucky you may see some crossbills whose preferred habitat is the Scots pine forest where they feed on the ripening cones. Your fortune may depend on whether the cone crop, which varies within a three or four year cycle, is good when you are there.*

The pleasant track continues with views across the loch; just over 1km after entering the forest a slender peninsula finger of old pines juts out from the shore and a small detour along it offers good views up and down Loch Ossian. Proceed along the track through the forest to the NE end of the loch, crossing a pretty river flowing into mixed woodland on the banks of the loch.

Cross two high stiles alongside gates in the deer fences to reach the area of Corrour Shooting Lodge. *At a track junction there is a memorial stone to Sir John Stirling Maxwell, a Director of the West Highland Railway (with an accolade perhaps seen as dubious by those who deplore the nature of much commercial forest planting!) which reads:*

"To commemorate Sir John Stirling Maxwell BT., 1866-1956 whose pioneer work on the planting of peat at Corrour led to the successful afforestation of large areas of Upland Britain. This memorial was unveiled by his daughter Mrs Anne Maxwell MacDonald on 21st Sept. 1967 when the Society of Foresters visited Corrour Forest."

The left-hand fork here heads down Strath Ossian towards Loch Laggan (see Walk 34). You turn right, however, and follow the track

Loch Ossian

around the end of the loch and past the present Corrour Shooting Lodge built to replace the old lodge destroyed by fire in 1942. *The estate comprises some 66,000 acres and includes several "Munros"; in its heyday it employed many staff and ran a steamer "Cailleach" on the loch. As recently as the 1930s the steamer plied between piers at each end of Loch Ossian, ferrying guests arriving by train, a horse drawn coach meeting them at the private station (then in the ownership of the estate), and transporting them the 1½km to the waiting steamer. Though the intricate romantic transport network has elapsed, the estate still accommodates parties for shooting and stalking from July to February.*

Cross the bridge over the River Ossian draining N to the River Spean and keep right at a fork to enter the forest across a stile. The track undulates through the trees before another stile brings you into more open woodland interspersed with rhododendrons including some unusual species. If you visit here in early summer you should be rewarded by some colourful blooms.

Emerging through a gate into open land the track follows the lochside towards some buildings on the shore near the site of the old steamer pier. Here is perhaps one of Scotland's remotest youth hostels, established in 1973 by a conversion of the former boathouse.

Continue on from the end of the loch, ignoring side tracks, towards the station with its scenic backdrop of Leum Villeim. There is only a small waiting room, the other old station buildings having been converted into a bunk house by the Morgans, the last station masters here, to service the walkers and climbers frequenting this superb area.

34. BEINN na LAP (937m) and STRATH OSSIAN from CORROUR

> SEE MAP I p136

ROUTE REVIEW

Station:	Corrour
Distance:	20km (12½ miles); 570m ascent
Grade:	Difficult/Serious
Maps:	OS Landranger 41 & 42
Terrain:	heather slopes, mountain ridges and gravel tracks
Estate:	Corrour (see Appendix B)
Refreshments:	None at all

Starting at Corrour Station (400m above sea level and once called Luibruaridh - pronounced Lebruary!), Beinn na Lap (mottled hill) is considered one of the easiest Munros to ascend by its south-west ridge. This walk continues down the north-east ridge to return to Corrour on gravel roads via Strath Ossian and the shore of Loch Ossian, giving an excellent full day's walk in remote country. Whilst we have graded it difficult/serious, it could well become a fully "serious mountain expedition" in bad weather conditions, and inexperienced hill walkers should only attempt this in good weather and be prepared to retrace their steps down the south-west ridge.

* * *

From Corrour Station set off E towards Loch Ossian; Beinn na Lap is clearly seen to the NE, and if the ground is reasonably dry it is possible to head N about 150 metres after the station across the flat area which is the watershed between Loch Ossian and Loch Treig, towards the lower part of Beinn na Lap's SW ridge. Alternatively, if you are not too confident of your footwear keeping your feet dry, continue down the track towards Loch Ossian for about 1km, then fork left and in a further 250 metres turn left again onto a minor track (The Road to the Isles) towards the W; after crossing a burn follow this uphill for almost 1km and then leave the track to climb N, again towards the lower part of Beinn na Lap's SW ridge.

From this ridge there are excellent views to the left (W) with Binnean Beag and the Mamores to the left of Glen Nevis, and Ben Nevis and the peaks of the Grey Corries to the right. Turn to the NE, up the ridge, which provides easy walking over short heather and springy turf; it becomes more rocky towards the top but remains at an easy angle. Beyond the parallel ridge of Garbh-bheinn leading to Meall Gharbh and Chno Dearg (Walk 35) on the left are seen the Easains, but Loch Treig remains hidden between. The summit cairn of Beinn na Lap is on the highest of the hummocky tops and, being a little apart from the other mountains, offers magnificent views roundabout; if you move just to the E of the summit there is a view down of the NE end of Loch Ossian.

To continue with the full walk (rather than returning directly to Corrour by the route of ascent) head NNE from the summit over stony ground to follow the ridge which points towards Creag Meagaidh in the distance across the Laggan Reservoir. Keep away from the right-hand side where there are cliffs - the ground features do tend to lead that way. *The valley on the left follows the line of a geological fault which continues to the NE through Lochan na h-Earba, from which it gets its name.* The ridge descends at a gentle angle for about 3km, but the end of it, above the valley of the Allt Feith Thuill, has been truncated and is quite steep. Keep a little to the right here, heading about NE, to find a way down the steep, mainly heather-clad slopes, avoiding small crags which are not easily seen from above. Do not be tempted to turn E or SE, however, across the ground where Loch na Lap is situated - this is an area of poorly drained peat-hags.

On reaching the valley a grassy track is followed E to join a gravel road at a bridge, about ³/₄km from Strathossian House hidden in trees further down the allt. Ahead is Loch Ghuilbinn and the wide Ossian flats, the floor of a great U-shaped valley carved by a glacier carrying ice northwards. Turning to the right, the gravel

Corrour Station for Walks 33, 34, 35 and 36

road leads beneath the cliffs of a spur, truncated by the glacier, and there is a similar feature on the opposite side of the valley. The road continues on the side of the valley, above the River Ossian, and in about 3¹/₂km enters the forest plantation around Corrour Lodge, close to the point where the Uisge Labhair flowing down from the bealach between Ben Alder and Aonach Beag joins the River Ossian. The first part of the forest has been felled, but replanting (and regeneration) are taking place. In about 300 metres a triangular track junction is reached; the route back to Corrour goes to the right, but a few metres along to the left is an interesting memorial to Sir John Stirling Maxwell (see Walk 33), and further to the left are stalkers houses and Corrour Lodge.

The track to Corrour goes through a gate, with a high stile alongside, and then passes through a pleasing mixture of coniferous trees alongside Loch Ossian (with some delightful spots on the shore to rest awhile). This is followed by a less interesting stretch of sitka plantation before open ground is reached. The track bends sharply left around the head of the loch and then meets the track leading from the station to the youth hostel. Turning right it is

1¹/₄km back to the station, and on a clear day you will be able to enjoy the fine views of Ben Nevis and its surrounding peaks ahead.

35. CORROUR to TULLOCH over CHNO DEARG (1047m) and STOB COIRE SGRIODAIN (976m)

SEE MAP I p136

ROUTE REVIEW

Stations:	Corrour, Tulloch
Distance:	23km (14¹/₂ miles); 860m ascent
Grade:	Serious
Map:	OS Landranger 41
Terrain:	high mountain terrain, remote, steep and rocky descent
Estate:	Corrour (see Appendix B)
Refreshments:	None; waiting room at Tulloch, but no seats!

NB. This walk can be shortened by omitting either Chno Dearg or Stob Coire Sgriodain; the latter also avoids the steep rocky descent and reduces the distance by 3km and the ascent by 100m

In walking north from Corrour there is a choice of two fine but demanding ridge walks, one on either side of Loch Treig which occupies a deep glacial trench. Here we have chosen to describe the ridge on the east side towering above the loch. This is a challenging route over remote mountain terrain with long snow-holding properties, but it is possible to shorten the expedition as indicated above. Whichever descent route is taken you proceed onwards to Tulloch Station by way of Fersit and the minor road from here to the A86.

Fersit was the site of much activity in the early 1930s when Loch Treig was dammed by British Alcan to supply water to generate electricity for their aluminium works at Fort William (see Walk 39). The water level in the loch was raised by some 10m and consequently the railway track had to undergo a more elevated realignment, its original route consigned beneath the water. In 1931 a station was established at Fersit where there was a camp for some 650 men involved in the construction of the dam and the tunnel to carry water to Fort William. It was closed again in January 1935, but evidence remains to be seen of the works complex which existed here in those years.

*   *   *

From Corrour Station cross to the W side of the line and follow the track (made by all-terrain vehicles) to the NW alongside the railway. You will come shortly to a sign-board marking the summit of the line (1350 feet, 408m) whilst on your left is Leum Villeim, a fine mountain though not quite a Munro, the highest point of the horseshoe above Coire a'Bhric Beag. In the next 1km the track crosses and re-crosses the burn from this corrie but, if the bridges are missing and it is not easily forded, it is possible to continue between it and the railway.

Immediately after crossing the bridge over a tributary, the Allt Luib Ruairidh (just over 2km from Corrour Station), where our track meets the The Road to the Isles, turn right to pass under the railway, where there was once an old cattle drovers' stance; from here strike up the hillside on the left, heading about NW to gain the SW ridge of Sron na Garbh-bheinne. The boggy grass on the lower slopes soon gives way to short heather. Follow the ridge NE and when the ground becomes fairly level veer to the left, still rising. A large cairn will be reached and it it is worth stopping here to identify some of the peaks which will be seen on this walk: *the impressive view of the Easains across Loch Treig will become a familiar sight; to their left there is a view up Glen Nevis with the Grey Corries, Aonach Beag and Ben Nevis on the right, Binnein Beag and the Mamores on the left; further to the left again are the much less spectacular hills towards the Blackwater Reservoir and the great expanse of Rannoch Moor.*

Continue on up the broad and hummocky ridge, amongst the perched blocks to which it owes its name, for another 2km to the summit of Garbh-bheinn (rough hill) from which the more defined ridge to Meall Garbh and Stob Coire Sgriodain beckons. There is a small descent at first along the ridge, which is almost parallel to the NE ridge of Beinn na Lap to the right, aligned with the Lochan na h-Earba fault (see Walk 34), but after crossing a line of fence posts the angle steepens up Meall Garbh and the route swings to the left. *From the top there are views to the east, across Loch Ghuilbinn and Strath*

Ossian, to what seems like range upon range of mountains dominated by Ben Alder, and Chno Dearg ahead can now be seen.

If the complete route is going to be more than all of the party can achieve before the train at Tulloch, now is the time to decide. There are two alternative ways in which it can be shortened.

Alternative a): by omitting Chno Dearg and proceeding directly to what we will call the second col between Meall Garbh and Stob Coire Sgriodain. For this head NW from the second (N) top of Meall Garbh.

Alternative b): by omitting Stob Coire Sgriodain and descending directly from Chno Dearg to the NNW on a direct line to Fersit. This has the advantage of avoiding the steep and rocky descent from Stob Coire Sgriodain.

To proceed to the summit of Chno Dearg (red nut) continue N from the second (N) top of Meall Garbh, swinging gradually round to NNE to the col here (the first col), but avoiding the steep drop into the corrie on the right. (These separate cols can be confusing in poor visibility, so take care.) From here go NE directly up the slope ahead to the flat summit of Chno Dearg. The fine views to the E are still available, but now you will also be able to see both Loch na Lap to the SE and N across Glen Spean.

If you are proceeding with the full round, return to the first col (noticing the crags on the E side of Meall Garbh), and from this col head just south of west to the second col. The ridge, which is littered with boulders, now leads WNW and there are two subsidiary tops to go over or round (but beware of the steep drops, at first to the right, but later to the left also) before the final climb to the top of Stob Coire Sgriodain (peak of the corrie of the scree). *Looking across the S end of Loch Treig on a clear day you will see to the hills of Glencoe, and Buachaille Etive Beag in particular stands out with a classical U-shaped glacial valley on its left, whilst Creag Meagaidh and other mountains are seen to the NNE across the Loch Laggan reservoir.*

It is now time to descend to Fersit, and this is where the most difficult part of the route is encountered. The ridge heads generally N and there is just one steep section before its "rough nose" (Sron Garbh). After that, however, there are steep and rocky sections and considerable care is needed for a safe descent; an escape to the corrie on the right might be preferred. Avoid following the Allt Fhearghas but keep heading N down steep heathery slopes, passing to the right of both a rocky knoll and a rocky spur (seen below) to reach a gate onto a lane at GR 356780, just beyond a shed.

Turn left along this lane, past the cottages of Fersit, to cross the railway line and such waters of the beautiful River Treig which are "allowed out" to flow down over rocks and through pools to join the River Spean (rather than be diverted for the British Aluminium Company). At this point, with some 5km still to go along road to Tulloch Station, you will perhaps be feeling tempted to write to ScotRail to ask them to re-open Fersit Station!

Immediately after crossing the River Treig keep left past a phone box and then in about 150 metres turn right on the metalled road. This minor road past Inverlair is attractive and passes beside a peaceful lochan amongst hummocks of glacial deposition, woodlands and fields; just after passing the farm at Inverlair a deep hollow, known as "the robbers' pit" and considered to be a "kettle" left by a lingering mass of ice at the end of the Ice Age, is seen on the left.

The road crosses the rocky gorge of the River Spean and then goes over the railway. Immediately after crossing the railway a gate will be seen into Dun Dearg forestry plantation with a track following the fence above the railway. This provides an alternative to going up to the main A86 road, but it cannot be recommended as it terminates in less than 1km leaving the walker to negotiate long heather, young trees and a network of drainage ditches for the final 600 metres or so to the station. One of the rewards when you reach the station is being able to look S from it and see the array of summits which you have just traversed, giving that glow of satisfaction which comes from a long, hard day, successfully completed.

36. CORROUR to SPEAN BRIDGE via LOCH TREIG and over the LAIRIG LEACACH

SEE MAPS I & J p136 & p148

ROUTE REVIEW

Stations:	Corrour, Spean Bridge
Distance:	24km (15 miles); 260m ascent
Grade:	Difficult
Map:	OS Landranger 41
Terrain:	tracks and paths through wild, remote country
Estates:	Killiechonate; Corrour (see Appendix B)
Refreshments:	Spean Bridge - Old Station Restaurant; Little Chef

There are two major routes through the mountains west of Loch Treig (forsaken loch) leading to the Spean valley or Fort William. They diverge at the head of Loch Treig, reached in about 6km from Corrour Station, mainly along the The Road to the Isles. That through Glen Nevis is longer and ends with an 11km road walk to Fort William; the only accommodation available en route, unless you are carrying a tent, is in bothies. The route we describe here is over the Lairig Leacach (pass of the flagstones), reaching a height of 510m between the Easains and the Grey Corries; it can be undertaken within a day, albeit a long demanding one.

Loch Treig Head used to be an important place, with a droving stance, a market and burying ground, but much of this was lost when the loch level was raised in the 1930s (see Walk 35). Loch Treig House which once stood here was, according to an old tale, the scene of a strange event. As shepherds were playing cards a stranger called and was invited to join in. He proved quite expert at their card games and then produced his own pack - of Tarot cards, offering to tell their fortunes. One was dealt "Death" and in his shock dropped the cards. As he retrieved them from the floor he saw their visitor had iron shod hooves instead of feet. He and his companions fled in terror from the "stranger", pursued by the Devil (for such they believed him to be), striking sparks on the rocks in his pursuit. The Devil was last seen heading up the Lairig Leacach, so beware!

The Lairig Leacach is part of the ancient "Thieves Road", a route taken by the clansmen of Lochaber to carry out lucrative plundering raids on their fellow countrymen in Moray; later it was a much-used cattle droving route. There is a bothy splendidly situated shortly before the highest point on the walk at the foot of the NE ridge of Stob Ban, and this is a delightful spot to take a rest or shelter. It is possible to make for Roy Bridge Station in Glen Spean but, as this involves crossing the river on stepping stones, we have chosen Spean Bridge Station as the destination.

* * *

The initial route from Corrour Station follows the track taken by the previous walk (35) for 2km to meet up with The Road to the Isles where it passes under the railway (at GR 342681). You will need to cross the Allt Luib Ruiaridh - there should be a bridge - and our track then joins The Road to the Isles and follows it left. As this track descends to Loch Treig there are magnificent views ahead of the Mamore Range dominated by Binnein Mor with Binnein Beag to its right. The track turns left alongside the loch with fine bridges over each of three rivers flowing into the loch. A footpath leads up into the wild Gleann Iolairean, and after crossing the third bridge there is a signpost at the footpath junction alongside Creaguaineach Lodge, a substantial habitation in this very remote location.

Here we leave the route to Glen Nevis and Fort William and keep right still following the loch shore. In about 300 metres, near to some sheep pens, there is a choice: a bridge down to the right crosses the Allt na Lairige or a path continues ahead; your choice here will decide whether you follow the E or the W side of the Allt na Lairige for the next 6km. The path is better on the W side, but that on the E side traverses the steep slope above the gorge eroded by the river between Creag Ghuanach and Creagan a'Chase and provides a view of the fine waterfall, Easan Dubh, dropping some 6m down the gorge; it also avoids the need to cross the Allt a'Chuil Choirean which could present considerable difficulty when in spate.

Either path offers a fine walk up the Lairig Leacach to the small bothy below Stob Choire Claurigh; that on the E side keeps well up on the valley side typically some 200 metres from the river, but is rather indistinct in parts. With the mighty Stob Coire Easain dominating its eastern side, the valley rises in a series of steps; more open sections into which the allt has been incised are separated by steeper parts where the river descends in waterfalls.

The bothy is magnificently situated beneath the Grey Corries close to the confluence of the Allt a'Chuil Choirean and the Allt na Lairige. (Contrary to the impression given by the OS map, the former carries more water.) Beyond the bothy there is a good Landrover track which leads on up to the summit of the lairig between Stob Coire na Ceannain on the left and the steep and rocky Sgurr Inse on the right. Once over the summit the track follows the Allt Leachdach down a valley of rock and heather to enter a forest plantation through a gate in a high deer fence almost 5km beyond the bothy.

The track winds down through the forest between larch trees and emerges on to rough pasture just above the line of the old narrow gauge railway used in the tunnel construction from Loch Treig to the hydroelectric turbines for the aluminium works at Fort William (see Walk 39). *The "central station" of this railway was located here with a turning triangle and passing loop, together with a hospital and canteen for the workforce.* The track continues down towards the

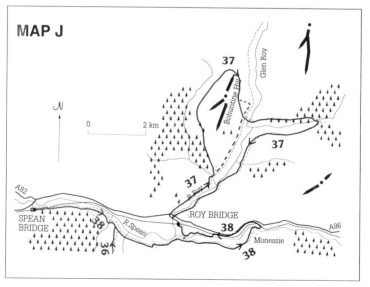

River Spean but just before reaching the first habitation it crosses a very flat area, perhaps the floor of an old ice-dammed lake. *The property here, Corriechoille, was once the home of John Cameron, a very prosperous drover in the nineteenth century whose cattle used the route you have just walked.*

The road (for that is what it has now become) swings left, past the farm, and then turns sharply right; from here, if you do not mind some boggy ground, you can take a green lane just below a fence which leads on through woods to rejoin the now metalled road at the bridge over The Cour. The final 3km alongside the River Spean to Spean Bridge Station is delightful through Scots pine and broad-leaved woodland, and there are opportunities to leave the road along small paths overlooking the river.

37. GLEN ROY and the PARALLEL ROADS from ROY BRIDGE

SEE MAP J p148

ROUTE REVIEW

Station:	Roy Bridge
Distance:	19km (12 miles); 450m ascent
Grade:	Moderate/Difficult
Map:	OS Landranger 41
Terrain:	hillsides with and without paths, together with tracks and minor road
Estates:	Forest Enterprise (Torlundy); Glen Roy National Nature Reserve; Glen Spean
Refreshments:	Roy Bridge - Inn; Stronlossit Hotel

N.B. This walk can be shortened by returning down the road on the west side of the River Roy reducing the distance by 5km and the ascent by 180m (and if the only bridge over the river is uncrossable it will be necessary to take this shorter alternative).

The fascinating features of the Parallel Roads of Glen Roy are the focal point of this walk from Roy Bridge Station. These features are seen following round a number of hillsides in the vicinity of Glen Spean, but are most developed in Glen Roy. They can best be described as terraces on the hillsides and occur at heights of 260m, 325m and 350m above the present sea level. In times gone by they were thought to have been perhaps hunting roads of the mythical Gaelic hero Fingal or of Scottish Kings. According to current thinking (the basis of which is due to the work of a Swiss, Louis Agassiz, in the mid nineteenth century!), they represent successive shores of an ancient lake held back by great plugs of ice at the end of the Ice Age about 10,000 years ago. As the ice melted and ice-dams were breached the waters were able to flow from the lake over successive cols in the hills, and each col is thus associated with a parallel road at a particular height. On the Ordnance Survey map they are shown by double broken lines, as for farm tracks and forest roads, but do not be deceived; whilst they are often clearly discernible as you look across onto a hillside, those which have not been utilised as paths or modern tracks are not always so obvious when you are on them, being sometimes discontinuous, often obstructed by forestry plantations and, being horizontal terraces lacking drains, they are often rather boggy.

Almost the entire glen after the first 3km is now deserted, but there is much evidence of earlier settlements and stories of battles fought here, including the Battle of Mulroy on 4th August 1688 in which the MacDonnells of Keppoch defeated the Mackintoshs on a nearby hill in what was said to be the last inter-clan battle fought in Scotland. Earlier in 1645

Commemorative Plaque, Glen Roy

150

the Marquess of Montrose led his troops through this glen to Inverlochy where he defeated the Duke of Argyll.

* * *

From Roy Bridge Station turn left and then left again along the A86 for about 300 metres; at the cross roads beyond the bridge over the River Roy take the minor road to the right, signed "Glen Roy 8 miles", passing the white Memorial Hall and St Margaret's Catholic Church on the left. The twisty lane flanked by silver birches ascends gently above the River Roy. There is a cairn on the right of the road commemorating the Battle of Mulroy.

After passing above a plantation on the right the road descends to cross a tributary burn tumbling down a steep gorge just before a side road to Bohuntinville. Turn left up here for about 200 metres, and after passing the first cottage on the left head across the grazing land half left and round a fenced enclosure to reach a gate in the fence above. Pass through this, cross a stream and head up the rough pasture which may be muddy at first, to the NE corner of the forest plantation on the left. Cross a low fence here and continue gradually uphill with the larch forest on the left. At the highest point of this plantation a further plantation will be seen ahead rising up to the right; make for the right-hand (uppermost) end of this, cross the fence at the corner just above the plantation and then over two burns before heading WNW above this plantation of pine and spruce - a faint path about 30 metres from the plantation gives easier going through the heather. From here there are fine views across Glen Spean; the Aonoch Mor ski development can be seen to the right of the Grey Corries.

The highest point of this plantation is about 360m above sea level, and the 326m parallel road, your next goal, is about 1km away, so descend gradually while traversing round the fairly steep hillside - there are various small (sheep?) paths which can be used. Parallel roads will be seen on the slopes across the valley to the NW and in due course on the slopes to the N. The 326m "road" is quite a broad terrace on the NW side of Bohuntine Hill and some 70m vertically above the valley floor, and when it is reached it should be recognised without too much difficulty. As it is followed round the N end of Bohuntine Hill it is interrupted in places by more recent features but by continuing at the same height it is soon found again. The "roads" on the W side of Leana Mhor, seen across Glen Roy from here, are particularly distinct.

After rounding the N end of Bohuntine Hill and heading S for about ³/₄km you will find yourself above a car park and viewpoint on the road up the Glen. Whilst you will have enjoyed much finer viewpoints from this walk you might be interested to descend to the car park to see an explanation of the parallel roads illustrated with diagrams on a display there. Alternatively you can start a more gradual descent from here, crossing a burn by some fenced enclosures around some tanks, and then descending directly to the road through the trees alongside a second burn. This should bring you to the road by the Chalice Stone, a flat-topped oblong boulder about ¹/₂m high with a carving of a chalice on the side, thought to have been used as an altar. (From the car park it is a walk of about ³/₄km down the road to this stone.)

From this point we describe two alternatives:

You can return down the minor road to Roy Bridge through the hamlet of Bohuntine with its old stone barns and past the lonely phone and post boxes. There are good views towards Aonach Mor opening up all the while on this gentle descent back through open grazing land, past the Bohuntinville turn, to reach the station in about 4¹/₂km.

Alternatively the walk can be continued into Gleann Glas Dhoire but this is dependent on the bridge across the River Roy just below the Chalice Stone being crossable - it was in 1992, but in 1993 we found it in need of repair and fenced off. The grassy track to it zigzags down the wooded slope from the Chalice Stone and it leads to a deserted dwelling, Cranachan, on the E side of the River Roy. From there head ENE up the broad ridge to a stone enclosure from which a farm track leads on in the same direction to a gate into the forest ahead.

From here a forest road leads uphill to join the line of the 260m parallel road and then follows this, remaining level for about 1km, before turning downhill to a gate and a bridge with a small hut just beyond. Our route turns sharply right and ascends alongside forest to join a track emerging from this forest constructed along the 260m parallel road. After keeping to this level for a little over 1km the track descends steadily to the hamlet of Bohenie directly across the Glen from Bohuntine. The impression gained here is that Bohenie must be too remote for the collection of large items of refuse! The walk back to Roy Bridge is now about 3km on a metalled road, often on a terrace with the river in an incised valley below.

38. SPEAN BRIDGE to ROY BRIDGE via MONESSIE GORGE

SEE MAP J p148

ROUTE REVIEW

Stations:	Spean Bridge, Roy Bridge
Distance:	13km (8 miles); 110m ascent
Grade:	Easy
Map:	OS Landranger 41
Terrain:	mostly good surfaced tracks and lanes; also a footpath, possibly muddy
Estate:	Killiechonate
Refreshments:	Roybridge - Inn; Stronlossit Hotel
	Monessie - Glen Spean Lodge

NB. It is possible to shorten this walk by some 7km, omitting Monessie Gorge and avoiding a stretch along the main road, by crossing directly to Roy Bridge using stepping stones over the River Spean; the road walk may also be avoided by returning from Monessie on the outward route.

This lovely route along Glen Spean is well worth doing (despite a short section along the road) for the enjoyment of following the River Spean through attractive woodland to the Braes of Lochaber where it cuts through the spectacular Monessie Gorge which can be seen from the train - all too briefly - and crossed by a suspension bridge on the walk. In 1895, *Mountain, Moor and Loch* described the Spean at Monessie as a "white torrent boiling down the rugged bed in a mad delirious ferment, forming a picture that seems an embodiment of the Highlands, proud, turbulent and untameable". Now, however, much of this water is diverted through a tunnel to the Fort William Aluminium Works' hydroelectric scheme (see Walks 35 & 39), though the gorge itself remains impressive.

Spean Bridge owes its location to the renowned Thomas Telford who constructed the present bridge here in 1819, replacing the earlier bridge over the Spean built by Wade some 3km to the west, Highbridge, the ruins of which still tower some 30m above the river.

This is MacDonell country, a clan reported by Wade as being among those "most addicted to rapine and plunder" and thus enlisted to support Prince Charles in waylaying the English at Highbridge in an opening skirmish of the '45. Near Roy Bridge Station stands Keppoch House, the seat of the MacDonell clan; there was once a castle here and the site of a motte and bailey nearby can be identified. In 1663 there was an horrific murder of two young nephews of the 13th Clan Chief, instigated in jealousy over the Chiefdom by MacDonald of Inverlair (near Tulloch). Retribution followed when he himself was slain together with his 6 sons. (For a graphic account, see *Mountain, Moor and Loch*.)

*   *   *

Turn right from Spean Bridge Station along the minor road following close by the River Spean. The road leads east, crosses over the railway and passes through mixed woodland with mainly oaks to the right and birch to the left. Keep left at a fork where a right turn goes to Killiechonate. After crossing a bridge, views of Beinn Chlianaig (721m) on the right open up and the metalled road ceases near a right fork signed "Corriechoille and Footpath to Rannoch", down which the route of Walk 36 from the Lairig Leacach descends.

Keep left here along a track with a Scout Trefoil sign. The track crosses the Allt Leachdach over a wooden (vehicular) bridge. Pass through a deer gate and on past the Scout buildings, following the riverside to Insh. Here you cross a burn and then turn left through a gate into a field following a track to a gate on the far side. Go through this and turn right on a farm track which continues through agricultural land until a ladder stile takes you into open woodland with the track following the river bank.

The track bends right over a wooden bridge; as you approach a white cottage immediately before a gate in the deer fencing there is a rough route down to the edge of the river and at this point you can make directly for Roy Bridge Station:

If the water level and a bit of courage permit, it is possible to cross the Spean on stepping stones to reach Roy Bridge on the far side - you might wish to acquire a stout stick to provide an additional point of balance! On reaching the far bank turn left and slightly away from the river on a small path through the woods which are full of flowers in spring. When you approach a ruined building pass to the left over a plank bridge and then head upwards and through a gate into a green lane which leads into the minor road to the station.

If you are continuing along to Monessie, follow the track through the gate to the right of the white cottage. The route rises up, and out onto open moorland away from the river which is seen below to your left. Keep ahead until you see a stone track rising more steeply to an old quarry dating back to the days of the old Lochaber Narrow Gauge Railway which ran along the hillside above Glen Spean (see Walk 39).

Turn left before the quarry track and continue on the farm track to Monessie Farm buildings. Pass through two gates, turning left after the farmhouse and follow the track through the fields. It winds gently down to the river which here meanders through a gravel bed prior to plunging down the gorge. At a fork keep left to reach the suspension bridge which takes you across Monessie Gorge with its brown water tumbling through the granite walls of the defile. *(Please note: the suspension bridge carries a warning sign "Danger Persons using this structure do so at their own risk British Alcan Highland Smelters Ltd.") The pipelines in the gorge are relics of a temporary hydroelectric scheme used during the building of the tunnel from Loch Treig to Fort William.*

After crossing the bridge turn right along the track, keeping left at a junction. Follow alongside the railway and over the railway bridge, then turn right along the track between the houses to reach the A86. *Almost immediately opposite, across the main road, a small track leads to the attractive little church of Cille Choirill, high above the road. For centuries the burial place of the MacDonells of Keppoch, its ruins were restored by local effort and the church reopened in 1932.*

Turn left on the A86; care should be exercised on the walk alongside the road, using the verge wherever possible and facing the oncoming traffic. In just under 2km and shortly after a new white bungalow on the left and a forestry track on the right, turn left towards the river on a grassy track into wooded land and cross over a railway bridge. The path through the wood follows a ridge above the river bank and can be muddy. However a network of minor paths thread their way between the river and the railway leading back towards Roy Bridge so you can pick the driest, easiest route to gain a track leading past some chalets and houses to the railway bridge. Roy Bridge Station is reached down steps to the left before crossing the bridge.

39. FORT WILLIAM to SPEAN BRIDGE through LEANACHAN FOREST

SEE MAP K p157

ROUTE REVIEW

Stations:	Fort William, Spean Bridge
Distance:	19km (12 miles); 350m ascent
Grade:	Moderate
Maps:	OS Landranger 41; OS Outdoor Leisure 32 (1:25,000)
Terrain:	mainly forest tracks; with little modification this route could be satisfactorily undertaken on a mountain bike
Estates:	Killiechonate; Forest Enterprise (Torlundy)
Refreshments:	Spean Bridge - Old Station Restaurant; Little Chef

Down the hillside to the NW of Fort William, on the lower slopes of Ben Nevis, run a set of massive pipes through which water flows to generate electricity in the power station at the aluminium works below. This walk crosses, and then follows below, the route of the narrow gauge railway built in 1925-6 to facilitate the construction of the tunnel which carries this water from Loch Treig and Loch Laggan to the portals at the top of the pipes. Although it was not originally intended to retain this light railway after the tunnel construction was completed, it in fact survived intact (with repairs and rebuilding) until a storm and landslip in 1971 carried away a bridge and section of the line; before then it had provided maintenance workers with access to the intake points for the tunnel from burns which it crossed. The railway was removed in stages from 1971 to 1976 as vehicle tracks were provided to the intake points, and sadly the route can no longer be followed as many bridges are missing or unsafe.

MAP K

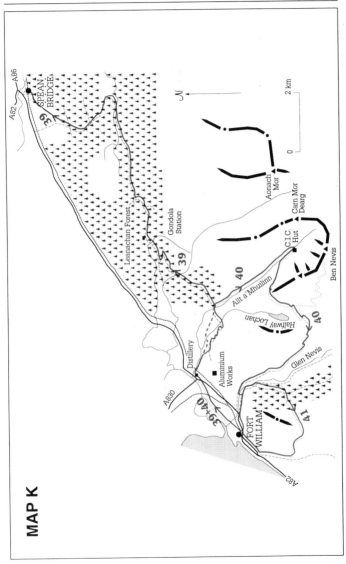

SPEAN BRIDGE

A86

A82

39

Leanachan Forest

Gondola Station

39

Aonach Mor

Carn Mor Dearg

C.I.C. Hut

Ben Nevis

40

Allt a' Mhuilinn

Halfway Lochan

40

Glen Nevis

41

Distillery

Aluminium Works

A830

39+40

FORT WILLIAM

A82

N

0   2 km

This walk also passes close to the bottom station of the Gondola opened in 1989 to develop the Aonach Mor ski area. Sadly again a proposal in 1974 to provide access to such a gondola lift by means of an electric railway from Fort William along the alignment of the old narrow gauge railway has not been implemented.

The walk proceeds to the Ben Nevis Distillery which has a visitor centre and offers guided tours with a wee dram; it then climbs steeply behind the aluminium works to reach the final intake point for the tunnel. After this it enters the forest and continues on forest roads providing easy walking to Leanachan, and then on a minor road towards Spean Bridge. Most of the route is suitable for mountain bikes and the steep climb can be avoided by proceeding to Torlundy on the A82 road (otherwise bikes may need to be lifted over gates on the forest roads).

*   *   *

The first goal on this walk is the Ben Nevis Distillery opposite the junction of the A82 and A830 roads. Whilst it can be reached from Fort William Station by a pavement alongside the main road, a more attractive alternative follows the River Lochy. Turning right out of the railway station you should see at the corner of the station building a signpost "Footpath to Inverlochy". Cross over a car park area and along the edge of a playing field to a bridge over the River Nevis. Cross the bridge and turn left immediately down some steps to follow a pathway, which is partly a raised boardwalk over the low-lying marshy ground along the banks of the River Lochy. *The shrubby wooded ground to your left here, enclosed by a meandering sweep of the river, was the site of the battles of Inverlochy in 1431 and 1645.*

Cross the narrow bridge which spans the water outlet from the aluminium works, and continue on underneath the railway bridge carrying the West Highland Line northwards to Mallaig. Around the corner are the ruins of Inverlochy Castle. Pass these on your right and follow the river bank to reach the road junction and the Distillery from which the Dew of Ben Nevis originates.

The onward route passes between the northern side of the distillery buildings and the Allt a'Mhuilinn (or "Whisky Burn") alongside it; proceed under the railway bridge and along a broad track with the burn on your left. It is necessary to cross two leats, the first carrying water back to the burn and the second leading water from a weir on the burn to a small reservoir, but it is usually fairly easy to step across these on concrete blocks. Immediately after the second crossing there is a stile over a fence; beyond this keep right to reach a Landrover track in about 300 metres. Turn left on this and follow it, zigzagging uphill. There are two turnings on the right (to access points on the water pipes) to avoid; after the second one the track leads more gently left and then a little downhill to an intake point from the Allt a'Mhuilinn to the water tunnel, marked by a substantial crane.

Cross the Allt a'Mhuilinn and continue up the track alongside it for about 100 metres where you turn left through a gate into a forestry plantation. This forest road at first ascends a little and there are excellent views from it through rides on the right to the North-East face of Ben Nevis, before it descends for about $^3/_4$km to a gate in a fence. From here the ski-lifts on the upper slopes of Aonach Mor can be seen and, much closer, a dam at the intake on the Allt na Caillich. Passing through the gate the track continues down to the NE through old workings associated with the water tunnel construction; *there was a horizontal adit just to the right of the track which was one of eleven access points for tunnel excavation, and this was connected to the narrow gauge railway below by a branch line which lead down to the ENE.*

Continue on down the track, crossing the Allt na Caillich and the line of the old railway, towards the lower gondola station which can be seen ahead, before swinging sharply left and down to join a forestry road below. Turn right along this, passing signs for various short walks from the gondola station, along the side of the car park and under the gondola cables. There has been substantial tree felling ahead with replanting, but some mature trees have been left. About 1km beyond the gondola station a track comes in on the right and in a further 300 metres you should turn right at a track crossing.

The forest is now thicker and more continuous, but it soon opens out on the left alongside the Allt an Loin and its tributaries. About 3km after the last turning avoid a new forest road on the left and proceed, past a minor green track on the right, to Leanachan where the road swings round to the left and becomes metalled. This continues as a pleasant road through dense forest, though some of the larch on the right has suffered considerably from wind damage. There is a green lane leading off to the right and then you cross a wide ride followed by a forest road before the road emerges from the forest into unfenced rough pasture.

The road leads down to the A82, but, if you prefer to avoid a final 1¹/₂km on the main road, head off towards the NE across the rough pasture to the NW corner of the forestry plantation. Crossing the fence alongside the plantation leads into the golf course, and following round the edge of this (with the forest on the right) for about ¹/₂km leads to the station at Spean Bridge.

40. C.I.C. HUT on BEN NEVIS via Allt a'MHUILINN from FORT WILLIAM

SEE MAP K p157

ROUTE REVIEW

Station:	Fort William
Distance:	18km (11 miles); 720m ascent
Grade:	Difficult
Maps:	OS Landranger 41; OS Outdoor Leisure 32 (1:25,000)
Terrain:	along mountain tracks and paths, but some may be very boggy
Estate:	Killiechonate
Refreshments:	After perhaps a wee dram at the Distillery, nothing else is available until you return to Fort William where there is plenty of choice

This walk takes you into some of the most impressive mountain scenery in Britain. The high point is the C.I.C. Hut, at about 680m magnificently situated beneath the mighty North-East face of Ben Nevis. It was built in the 1920s in memory of Captain Charles Inglis Clark who died of wounds received in Mesopotamia in 1918, and now provides accommodation in this excellent situation for members of the Scottish Mountaineering Club and their guests. Please note that it does not offer any facilities at all for day visitors.

Our path to it is that generally taken by climbers destined for the big mountaineering routes and the formidable climbs on the cliffs which tower above it. In times gone by they too walked up past the Distillery and enjoyed the intoxicating aroma around it, but now most find more convenient places to leave their cars. From the C.I.C. Hut we traverse round the N side of Ben Nevis on a path which can be very exposed in bad weather, and where avalanches have occurred, to join the "Tourist Track" near the Halfway Lochan for the return to Fort William.

Although we have only graded this walk Difficult, Ben Nevis is a mountain to be taken very seriously. There are stories of hardened climbers taking almost 24 hours to reach the C.I.C. Hut from Fort William in severe weather, so do not undertake this walk unless you are fully prepared for the conditions which you might encounter. For those wanting a much shorter route, the walk up to the Allt a'Mhuilinn intake and back (two alternative routes are described and one could be used there and the other for the return), would be appropriate.

* * *

Proceed to the Ben Nevis Distillery using the route described in Walk 39 and continue between the N side of the distillery buildings and the burn alongside; after going under a railway bridge and crossing two leats, there is a stile over a fence and then a choice of routes:

The easier and more straightforward route keeps right to reach a Landrover track in about 300 metres. This is the route described in Walk 39 and leads to an intake point from the Allt a'Mhuilinn, marked by a substantial crane.

The alternative route, keeping left after the stile, leads across wet ground (with some slippery boards across particularly wet parts) to a wider track in about 400 metres (this is the track of the old narrow gauge railway - see Walk 39). Follow this to the left, crossing a small burn by a bridge and then fork right and right again to follow fainter paths up the bracken slopes and wooded hillside to join the Landrover track just before the intake point after about $^3/_4$km of fairly steep climbing.

Cross the Allt a'Mhuilinn and continue a further 250 metres along the Landrover track on its E side, (avoiding the turning which leads left into the forest - Walk 39), to its end and a stile over the fence. Along this stretch the views are opening up of Coire Leis ahead and the magnificent North-East face of Ben Nevis. If this is as far as you wish to go, you can return from here, but it is easier to follow the Landrover track down to the distillery than to try to locate the rather faint path from the top.

Ahead the route proceeds up the glen of the Allt a'Mhuilinn. For the first few hundred metres the path has been drained and surfaced, but it soon deteriorates, and after wet weather can be very boggy for about 2km. There are indicator posts with red markers which can be followed, but a more attractive and perhaps slightly drier path keeps closer to the allt. After crossing a burn coming down from Carn Beag Dearg on the left, the floor of the glen begins to rise, the Allt a'Mhuilinn tumbles down in a series of waterfalls and the path becomes drier as it climbs over glacial morainic material.

About 3½km after crossing the stile you reach the C.I.C Hut by crossing the burn which descends from Coire Leis. *Its situation is superb, located directly below Coire na Ciste which is bounded on its left by the mighty Tower Ridge rising from the massive Douglas Boulder virtually to the summit of Ben Nevis and on its right by the Great Buttress of Carn Dearg; gullies which provide fine winter climbing routes onto The Ben can just be seen at the head of Coire na Ciste. To the right of Carn Dearg is Castle Ridge, whilst to the left of Tower Ridge are Observatory Ridge and the North-East Buttress, and at the head of Coire Leis is the Carn Mor Dearg Arête (not to be confused with Carn Dearg!) which provides a very fine route to the summit of The Ben for the competent scrambler.*

Our route descends about 100 metres from the C.I.C Hut to cross the burn coming down from Coire na Ciste and then follows down the left-hand side of the Allt a'Mhuillin along a path below the Great Buttress of Carn Dearg which provides a fine view up Castle Ridge. After about ½km the path diverges from the allt and traverses the slopes beneath Castle Ridge. It descends a little at first but then begins to climb steadily over boulders offering fine views down and across the glen climbed earlier. Eventually the path swings round to the left and from here there are views ahead across the outskirts of Fort William to Loch Eil. The North-East face of The Ben is now left behind and after crossing a line of old fence posts the path heads SW and S with Lochan Meall an t-Suidhe (or the Halfway Lochan) on the right. About ¾km after passing the fence posts, a smaller path leads right to join the Ben Nevis Tourist Track which we follow down. (If this small path is missed, the Tourist Track itself is met about 150 metres further on after a short ascent.) *This track was originally constructed as a pony track to the summit observatory, which was built in 1883 and from where hourly observations were made for 21 years.*

The track zigzags down into a somewhat enclosed valley and then continues down round the hillside with views into Glen Nevis and of the western end of the Mamore Range. *(Further zigzags in the track enable these views to be appreciated without stopping to turn round!) The track here has recently been improved, using pitching techniques with the local stone, establishing drainage and providing aluminium bridges over burns.* At the corner of a fence around young trees a path leads down to the youth hostel in Glen Nevis, but we continue ahead down an easier gradient.

From Achintee House the small road down the E side of Glen Nevis is followed, alongside green fields. After passing a transformer station on your right and the Town Park you will see a green tubular bridge across the river on your left. Cross over this and take the pavement along the W side of the glen to reach a roundabout on the A82 alongside a woollen shop and restaurant. Turn left here and follow the main road back to the station.

41. THE PEAT TRACK from FORT WILLIAM

SEE MAP K p157

ROUTE REVIEW

Station:	**Fort William**
Distance:	**10km (6 miles); 220m ascent**
Grade:	**Moderate**
Maps:	**OS Landranger 41; OS Outdoor Leisure 32 (1:25,000)**
Terrain:	**minor roads, clear track and path (may be muddy)**
Estate:	**Forest Enterprise (Torlundy)**
Refreshments:	**Tearooms/restaurants in Glen Nevis and plenty of selection in Fort William**

Fort William takes its name from a fort constructed in 1655 by

General Monck, which became the base for attempts to bring to heel those clans hostile to the English King. Hence many Highlanders objected to the name and Fort William became known variously as Duncansburgh, Gordonsburgh and Maryburgh and there have been moves to rename it Invernevis. The fort was largely demolished in the building of the West Highland Railway locomotive depot. However, for some 40 years longer, the Governor's Room, where the order for the massacre of Glencoe was signed in 1692, was retained intact. Now, part of this room is reconstructed in the West Highland Museum in the High Street.

Our walk goes up Glen Nevis, the subject of a gloomy poem penned in the sixteenth century:

> Glen Nevis, a glen of stones,
> A glen where corn ripens late,
> A long, wild, waste glen
> With thieving folk of evil habit.

In the past it was the scene of illegal distilling which enabled the poor crofters to pay their rent; our route continues over the moors, following the "Peat Track" which local people used to fetch peat to dry for fuel. It offers superb views of the surrounding mountains and can readily be managed between trains while leaving sufficient time if wished for a good browse along the High Street.

* * *

From the station turn left to follow the A82 in an easterly direction towards Spean Bridge and the Great Glen. You pass the hospital and Lochaber Leisure Centre on your right and in about 1km reach a roundabout where the minor road to Glen Nevis goes ahead, with the A82 swinging left to cross the River Nevis. Take the Glen Nevis road (there is a pavement), which follows alongside the river on its course down the glen. Shortly after a bend southwards in the road there is a small sign ("Private Fishing") on a tree alongside the river; here the Nevis tumbles through a small gorge and it's easy to imagine salmon leaping at this spot. About 1km after the roundabout a Forestry Commission notice on the right side of the road signals the start of Nevis Forest and shortly after this you leave the road, turning right through a gate onto a forest track which passes between mature forest to the left and a recently cleared and replanted area to the right. As the track bends round left, views open up to the head of Glen Nevis and, to the left, the massive bulk of Ben Nevis. The so-called "Tourist Track" (the descent in Walk 40) can be seen wending its way diagonally over the shoulder from Achintee across the glen.

The forest track rises easily ahead, passing two ancient walled cemeteries of the Clan Cameron on the left, until it reaches a point where the West Highland Way (see the thistle symbol on the post) comes up from the left to continue along the forest road ahead. Our route, however, turns right on the signed "Peat Track to Achintore", a small but distinct path which climbs fairly steeply up the hillside through larch and birch wood. The path is stony but firm, though there may be some water running down. Rewarding views can be seen over your right shoulder to distant peaks, whilst the Ben Nevis range continues to dominate across the glen to your rear.

As the gradient eases you emerge from the forest adjacent to a fence running from Cow Hill on the right, southwards towards Beinn Riabhach. Cross the fence via the gate and continue heading W over the moor. It is softer going here; the peaty path crosses a plateau some 200m above sea level to reach a recently cut wide track where there is a large cairn to the left and a sign indicating "Peat Track to Glen Nevis" along the path you have come. Keep left on this wide track which descends easily past another couple of cairns to Upper Achintore on the outskirts of Fort William. *It is hard to believe that Loch Linnhe separates you from the peaks ahead but you will soon see Corpach (marking the start of the Caledonian Canal) on the far bank to the right where Loch Linnhe and Loch Eil meet.*

Continue down to where the Peat Track meets a metalled road; turn right on this, past a cattle grid to follow Lundavra Road down past some housing to the town. At the roundabout, either the road alongside Loch Linnhe or the High Street, with the Tourist Information Centre and the West Highland Museum (both in the Square), will take you back to the railway station.

APPENDIX A:
TABLE of WALKS Classified by Grade

Number	Title	Distance km	Ascent m	Page
SERIOUS				
5	The Cobbler, Beinn Narnain and A'Chrois from Arrochar & Tarbet	19	1410	35
8	Ardlui to Arrochar & Tarbet over Ben Vorlich and via Glen Loin	16	1110	46
10	Ardlui to Tyndrum over Ben Oss	22	1260	54
11	An Caisteal and Beinn a'Chroin from Crianlarich	18	990	56
12	Cruach Ardrain from Crianlarich	12	1050	59
15(b)	Tyndrum to Dalmally over Ben Lui and Beinn a'Chleibh	21	1110	70
18	Dalmally Horseshoe including Stob Diamh from Loch Awe	14	1000	78
19	Beinn Eunaich and Beinn a'Chochuill from Loch Awe	19	1164	80
22	Taynuilt to Falls of Cruachan (or Loch Awe) over Ben Cruachan	(23) 18	1200	89 89
27(b)	Tyndrum to Bridge of Orchy via Auch Gleann and over Beinn Dorain	20	970	110
28	Beinn an Dothaidh from Bridge of Orchy	14	810	112
35	Corrour to Tulloch over Chno Dearg and Stob Coire Sgriodain	23	860	142
DIFFICULT/SERIOUS				
2	Garelochhead to Arrochar & Tarbet over Doune Hill	24	1290	25
3	Ben Reoch, Beinn Bhreac and Tullich Hill from Arrochar & Tarbet	15	1030	30
27(a)	Tyndrum to Bridge of Orchy over Beinn Odhar	12	630	109
32(b)	Rannoch to Corrour over Carn Dearg	20	670	134
34	Beinn na Lap and Strath Ossian from Corrour	20	570	139

(NB. At the time of writing changes were taking place in telephone numbers within this area, so there may be some changes to the information below; new numbers where known are in brackets.)
ESTATES with CONTACT ADDRESSES and REQUESTS concerning ACCESS (in alphabetical order)

ARGYLL FOREST PARK
Forest Enterprise,
Kilmun by Dunoon,
Argyll PA23 8SE
0136 984 666

AUCH
C.Macdonald
Auch, Tyndrum
01838 400233

AUCHREOCH (Coille Coire Chuilc)
M.M.Cruickshank of Auchreoch,
Auchreoch, Crianlarich,
Perthshire
01838 400218

BANNACHRA MUIR
Tilhill Economic Forestry,
Sauchieburn, Stirling
01786 811721

BEN LUI NATIONAL NATURE RESERVE
SNH Area Officer (Lorne)
Glensalloch Road,
Barcaldine, Oban PA37 1SF
0163172 363

BLACK CORRIES
Peter O'Connell,
Black Corries Estate
0185 56 272 (0855 851272)
Stalking and culling take place between September and 15th February. Please make contact before going on the hill in this period.

BLACKMOUNT
Hamish Menzies
01838 400225
or Ian Macrae
01838 400269
Dogs discouraged. Please leave hills quiet in September and first half of October (stag cull). No restriction on West Highland Way.

CASTLES FARM
Lochawe, Dalmally
Argyll

CONONISH
J.Burton
Cononish Farm,
Tyndrum

CORROUR
Ted Piggott
Head Stalker
Corrour Estate
0139 785 200
Please use paths when possible and
avoid estate during stalking season
unless access has been agreed with
the stalker.

DALMALLY
Tilhill Economic Forestry Ltd
Claremont, Glencruitten Road,
Oban, Argyll.
01631 62906 (01631 562906)

DUNAN
Colin Robertson,
Stalker's Cottage, Dunan Lodge,
Rannoch Station, Pitlochry
Perthshire PH17 2QD
01882 633266

FOREST ENTERPRISE (LORNE)
Millpark Road, Oban,
Argyll PA34 4NH
01631 66155 (01631 566155)

FORESTENTERPRISE
(TORLUNDY)
Fort William PH33 6SW
01397 702184

GLENFALLOCH
D.Neilson,
Clisham Cottage, Glen Falloch
013014 229 (01301 400229)
No dogs please. Access may be
restricted during the stalking
season (except on the West
Highland Way)

GLENKINGLASS
Tim Healy, Stalker,
Ardmaddy, Taynuilt, Argyll
0186 62 271 (01866 200271)

GLENOE
Mr Ian Stewart,
Glenoe, Taynuilt, Argyll
0186 62 212 (01866 200212)

GLEN ROY NATIONAL NATURE
RESERVE
SNH Area Officer,
Mamore House, The Parade,
Fort William PH33 6BA
01397 704716

GLEN SPEAN
Mr Luxmore
0139 781 558

GLENSTRAE
Derek Dempster,
Duiletter Bungalow
0183 82 217

INVERUGLAS
Mr John Duncan
Inveruglas Farm, by Arrochar
G83 7DP
0130 14 210 (01301 400210)
No dogs please and avoid
disturbing sheep during the
lambing season (April and May)

KILLIECHONATE
West Highland Estates Office,
33 High Street, Fort William
01397 2433

LOCHS
W Mason,
Croc-na-Keys, Lochs Estate,
Glen Lyon, Aberfeldy
01887 866 224

LUSS
Luss Estates Company,
Arden, Dunbartonshire
01389 850642

RANNOCH DEER
MANAGEMENT ASSOC.
Nicholas Thexton,
Gaur Cottage,
by Rannoch Station
01882 633248

SLOY
Scottish Hydro Electric plc
16 Rothesay Terrace,
Edinburgh EH3 7SE
Local Contact: Sloy Power Station
0130 14 245 (01301 400245)

STRATHFILLAN
Fountain Forestry,
Perth
01738 38425 (01738 638425)

STUCKENDROIN
Mr James Fisher,
Stuckendroin Farm, Ardlui
013014 283 (01301 400283)
No dogs please and avoid
disturbing sheep during the
lambing season (April and May)

OTHER USEFUL ADDRESSES

Tourist Information Centres
* Helensburgh: Clock Tower, The Pier (01436) 672742
* Tarbet: Main Street (013012) 260 (01301 200260)
* Tyndrum: Main Street (01838) 400246
  Oban: Argyll Square (01631) 63122 (01631 563122)
* Spean Bridge: Main Street; (01397) 712576
  Fort William, Cameron Centre, Cameron Square (01397) 703781

* *seasonal opening only (April to October)*

Scottish Rights of Way Society: John Cotton Business Centre, 10/2 Sunnyside,
   Edinburgh EH7 5RA
Scottish Youth Hostels Association: 7 Glebe Crescent, Stirling, FK8 2JA
   (01786) 451181
Scotrail: Caledonian Chambers, 87 Union Street, Glasgow, G1 3TA
   (0141 204) 2844
Post Bus: Post Office Customer Services (0131 228) 740

BIBLIOGRAPHY

Aitken, R: *Official Guide to the West Highland Way* HMSO 1990

Ang, T & Pollard, M: *Walking the Scottish Highlands - General Wade's Military Roads* André Deutsch 1984

Bennett, D: *The Munros - The Scottish Mountaineering Club Guide* Scottish Mountain Trust 1986

Bennett, D: *The Southern Highlands - Scottish Mountaineering Club District Guide* Scottish Mountain Trust 1986

Case Publications (with Scotrail): *The Official Guide to the West Highland Line* 1993

Crocket, K: *Ben Nevis - Britain's Highest Mountain* Scottish Mountain Trust 1986

Cunningham, A D: *The History of Rannoch* A.D.Cunningham 1984

Cunningham, A D: *Tales of Rannoch* A.D.Cunningham 1989

Famedram: reprint of *The Story of the West Highland (1940s LNER Guide)* Howat, P: *The Lochaber Narrow Guage Railway* Famedram 1980

HMSO: *The Climate of Scotland* 1989

Hodkiss, P: *The Central Highlands - Scottish Mountaineering Club District Guide* Scottish Mountaineering Trust 1984

Hunter, T: *A Guide to the West Highland Way* Constable 1979

MacDonald, M: *The Glens of Upper Lochaber* Oban Times 1990

Mountaineering Council of Scotland & Scottish Landowners Federation: *Heading for the Scottish Hills* Scottish Mountain Trust 1993

Mountain, Moor & Loch - on the Route of the West Highland Railway (1895) Sir Joseph Causton 1895

Sissons, J B: *The Geomorphology of the British Isles - Scotland* Methuen & Co Ltd. 1976

Storer, R: *Exploring Scottish Hill Tracks* David & Charles 1991

Thomas, J: *The West Highland Railway* David & Charles 1984

Weir, T: *Weir's Way* Gordon Wright Publishing 1981

Wittow, J B: *Geology and Scenery in Scotland* Penguin 1977

CICERONE GUIDES

Cicerone publish a wide range of reliable guides to walking and climbing in Britain, and other general interest books.

LAKE DISTRICT - General Books
A DREAM OF EDEN
LAKELAND VILLAGES
LAKELAND TOWNS
REFLECTIONS ON THE LAKES
OUR CUMBRIA
THE HIGH FELLS OF LAKELAND
CONISTON COPPER A History
LAKELAND - A taste to remember (Recipes)
THE LOST RESORT? (Morecambe)
CHRONICLES OF MILNTHORPE
LOST LANCASHIRE (Furness area)
THE PRIORY OF CARTMEL

LAKE DISTRICT - Guide Books
CASTLES IN CUMBRIA
THE CUMBRIA CYCLE WAY
WESTMORLAND HERITAGE WALK
IN SEARCH OF WESTMORLAND
CONISTON COPPER MINES Field Guide
SCRAMBLES IN THE LAKE DISTRICT
MORE SCRAMBLES IN THE LAKE DISTRICT
SHORT WALKS - SOUTH LAKELAND
WINTER CLIMBS IN THE LAKE DISTRICT
WALKS IN SILVERDALE/ARNSIDE
BIRDS OF MORECAMBE BAY
THE EDEN WAY
WALKING ROUND THE LAKES

NORTHERN ENGLAND (outside the Lakes
BIRDWATCHING ON MERSEYSIDE
CANAL WALKS Vol 1 North
CANOEISTS GUIDE TO THE NORTH EAST
THE CLEVELAND WAY & MISSING LINK
THE DALES WAY
DOUGLAS VALLEY WAY
HADRIANS WALL Vol 1 The Wall Walk
HERITAGE TRAILS IN NW ENGLAND
THE ISLE OF MAN COASTAL PATH
IVORY TOWERS & DRESSED STONES (Follies)
THE LANCASTER CANAL
LANCASTER CANAL WALKS
LAUGHS ALONG THE PENNINE WAY
A NORTHERN COAST-TO-COAST
NORTH YORK MOORS Walks
THE REIVERS WAY (Northumberland)
THE RIBBLE WAY
ROCK CLIMBS LANCASHIRE & NW
THE YORKSHIRE DALES A walker's guide
WALKING IN THE SOUTH PENNINES
WALKING IN THE NORTH PENNINES
WALKS IN THE YORKSHIRE DALES (3 VOL)
WALKS IN LANCASHIRE WITCH COUNTRY
WALKS IN THE NORTH YORK MOORS
WALKS TO YORKSHIRE WATERFALLS (2 vol)
WALKS ON THE WEST PENNINE MOORS
WALKING NORTHERN RAILWAYS (2 vol)
WALKING IN THE WOLDS

DERBYSHIRE & EAST MIDLANDS
WHITE PEAK WALKS - 2 Vols
HIGH PEAK WALKS
WHITE PEAK WAY
KINDER LOG
THE VIKING WAY
THE DEVIL'S MILL / WHISTLING CLOUGH (Novels)

WALES & WEST MIDLANDS
THE RIDGES OF SNOWDONIA
HILLWALKING IN SNOWDONIA
HILL WALKING IN WALES (2 Vols)
ASCENT OF SNOWDON
WELSH WINTER CLIMBS
SNOWDONIA WHITE WATER SEA & SURF
SCRAMBLES IN SNOWDONIA
SARN HELEN Walking Roman Road
ROCK CLIMBS IN WEST MIDLANDS
THE SHROPSHIRE HILLS A Walker's Guide
HEREFORD & THE WYE VALLEY A Walker's Guide
THE WYE VALLEY WALK

SOUTH & SOUTH WEST ENGLAND
COTSWOLD WAY
EXMOOR & THE QUANTOCKS
THE KENNET & AVON WALK
THE SOUTHERN-COAST-TO-COAST
SOUTH DOWNS WAY & DOWNS LINK
SOUTH WEST WAY - 2 Vol
WALKING IN THE CHILTERNS
WALKING ON DARTMOOR
WALKERS GUIDE TO DARTMOOR PUBS
WALKS IN KENT
THE WEALDWAY & VANGUARD WAY

SCOTLAND
THE BORDER COUNTRY - WALKERS GUIDE
SCRAMBLES IN LOCHABER
SCRAMBLES IN SKYE
THE ISLAND OF RHUM
CAIRNGORMS WINTER CLIMBS
THE CAIRNGORM GLENS (Mountainbike Guide)
THE ATHOLL GLENS (Mountainbike Guide)
WINTER CLIMBS BEN NEVIS & GLENCOE
SCOTTISH RAILWAY WALKS
TORRIDON A Walker's Guide
SKI TOURING IN SCOTLAND

REGIONAL BOOKS UK & IRELAND
THE MOUNTAINS OF ENGLAND & WALES
    VOL 1 WALES VOL 2 ENGLAND
THE MOUNTAINS OF IRELAND
THE ALTERNATIVE PENNINE WAY
THE PACKHORSE BRIDGES OF ENGLAND
THE RELATIVE HILLS OF BRITAIN
LIMESTONE - 100 BEST CLIMBS

Also a full range of EUROPEAN and OVERSEAS guidebooks - walking, long distance trails, scrambling, ice-climbing, rock climbing.

Other guides are constantly being added to the Cicerone List.
Available from bookshops, outdoor equipment shops or direct (send s.a.e. for price list) from
CICERONE, 2 POLICE SQUARE, MILNTHORPE, CUMBRIA, LA7 7PY

CICERONE GUIDES

Cicerone publish a wide range of reliable guides to walking and climbing abroad

FRANCE
TOUR OF MONT BLANC
CHAMONIX MONT BLANC - A Walking Guide
TOUR OF THE OISANS: GR54
WALKING THE FRENCH ALPS: GR5
THE CORSICAN HIGH LEVEL ROUTE: GR20
THE WAY OF ST JAMES: GR65
THE PYRENEAN TRAIL: GR10
THE RLS (Stevenson) TRAIL
TOUR OF THE QUEYRAS
ROCK CLIMBS IN THE VERDON
WALKS IN VOLCANO COUNTRY (Auvergne)
WALKING THE FRENCH GORGES (Provence)
FRENCH ROCK

FRANCE / SPAIN
WALKS AND CLIMBS IN THE PYRENEES
ROCK CLIMBS IN THE PYRENEES

SPAIN
WALKS & CLIMBS IN THE PICOS DE EUROPA
WALKING IN MALLORCA
BIRDWATCHING IN MALLORCA
COSTA BLANCA CLIMBS
ANDALUSIAN ROCK CLIMBS
THE WAY OF ST JAMES

FRANCE / SWITZERLAND
THE JURA - Walking the High Route and
  Winter Ski Traverses
CHAMONIX TO ZERMATT The Walker's
  Haute Route

SWITZERLAND
WALKING IN THE BERNESE ALPS
CENTRAL SWITZERLAND
WALKS IN THE ENGADINE
WALKING IN TICINO
THE VALAIS - A Walking Guide
THE ALPINE PASS ROUTE

GERMANY / AUSTRIA / EASTERN EUROPE
THE KALKALPEN TRAVERSE
KLETTERSTEIG - Scrambles
WALKING IN THE BLACK FOREST
MOUNTAIN WALKING IN AUSTRIA
WALKING IN THE HARZ MOUNTAINS
WALKING IN THE SALZKAMMERGUT
KING LUDWIG WAY
HUT-TO-HUT IN THE STUBAI ALPS
THE HIGH TATRAS

ITALY & SLOVENIA
ALTA VIA - High Level Walks in the Dolomites
VIA FERRATA - Scrambles in the Dolomites
ITALIAN ROCK - Rock Climbs in Northern Italy
CLASSIC CLIMBS IN THE DOLOMITES
WALKING IN THE DOLOMITES
THE JULIAN ALPS

MEDITERRANEAN COUNTRIES
THE MOUNTAINS OF GREECE
CRETE: Off the beaten track
TREKS & CLIMBS IN WADI RUM, JORDAN
THE ATLAS MOUNTAINS
WALKS & CLIMBS IN THE ALA DAG (Turkey)

OTHER COUNTRIES
ADVENTURE TREKS - W. N. AMERICA
ADVENTURE TREKS - NEPAL
ANNAPURNA TREKKERS GUIDE
CLASSIC TRAMPS IN NEW ZEALAND
TREKKING IN THE CAUCAUSUS

GENERAL OUTDOOR BOOKS
THE HILL WALKERS MANUAL
FIRST AID FOR HILLWALKERS
MOUNTAIN WEATHER
MOUNTAINEERING LITERATURE
THE ADVENTURE ALTERNATIVE
MODERN ALPINE CLIMBING
ROPE TECHNIQUES IN MOUNTAINEERING
MODERN SNOW & ICE TECHNIQUES
LIMESTONE -100 BEST CLIMBS IN BRITAIN

CANOEING
SNOWDONIA WILD WATER, SEA & SURF
WILDWATER CANOEING
CANOEIST'S GUIDE TO THE NORTH EAST

CARTOON BOOKS
ON FOOT & FINGER
ON MORE FEET & FINGERS
LAUGHS ALONG THE PENNINE WAY

*Also a full range of guidebooks
to walking, scrambling, ice-climbing,
rock climbing, and other adventurous
pursuits in Britain and abroad*

*Other guides are constantly being added to the Cicerone List.
Available from bookshops, outdoor equipment shops or direct (send for price list)
from CICERONE, 2 POLICE SQUARE, MILNTHORPE, CUMBRIA, LA7 7PY*

Printed by CARNMOR PRINT & DESIGN
95-97 LONDON ROAD, PRESTON, LANCASHIRE, UK.